THERE IS ALWAYS ROOM FOR ONE MORE

The Stockton Story (Aired July 10th, 2021, News Channel 7 WJLA Washington, DC)

ISBN

eBook 9798885253932

Paperback 9798885253949

Audio 9798885253833

There Is Always Room For One More

Before foster care, there were orphanages. The Orphan
Train Movement was a supervised welfare program that
transported children from crowded Eastern cities of the
United States to foster homes largely located in rural areas
of the Midwest. The orphan trains operated between 1854
and 1929, relocating about 250,000 children, (history.com).
Orphan trains brought children from New York City to
work on farms out West and over a seventy-five-year
period, up to 200,000 children went from city to farm. The
system could not accommodate all the homeless children;
many left on their own.
There are many stories of deprivation and abuse to tell from
that era of time. Orphanages began phasing out in the
1920s. Many charities created foster care agencies. "The
Depression years of 1920 and 1921 depleted the institutions
resources and forced the agencies to place children in foster
care homes, (Encyclopedia of Children and Childhood in
History and Society, 2014)."
The foster care system today has many cracks in its walls.
The system places too many poor and minority children
into the foster care system who could be kept at home.
Children are shuffles between multiple foster homes and
institutions, and I believe, placed on medications that are
not needed. This further traumatizes the children.
Unexpected changes that the child must go through because
of nothing they have done.

   As many as 70 percent of youths in the juvenile justice
system have been in the welfare system. Children usually
age out of their programs when they turn eighteen years of
age. However, there is no set age that marks the end of
foster care for some. Federal guidelines are in place to help
children during their transition from foster care to
independent living. The children who are aged out become

ineligible to receive state assistance with housing, food, and medical care under the foster care system. The federal government recognizes that all of these factors cause the children to suffer more. The lack of a stable home environment while growing up and depending on the system to survive can be drastic. Much of this causes emancipated young adults to experience higher rates of drug and alcohol abuse, mental instability, become suicidal, teen pregnancy, homelessness and increased arrest.

We need to work on our foster care programs by educating the public about foster care, strengthen the families of origin, help the children to function in foster care without drugging them with medication to control them, we need to support care workers and managers for they have a heavy workload, we need to help the children to build positive connections before they age out. We are all in this together for these children will one day be adults who are the future of our country. Remember, *there is always room for one more.*

<u>**Table of Contents**</u>

DEDICATION

If it were not for foster children, we would not have any stories to share with you. Foster children become foster children usually due to no fault of their own. There are an estimated 400,000 children (about half the population of Delaware) in the 50 foster care systems across the United States. In this book we will share our foster care stories, good and not so good with the reader; however, always rewarding. We will only use first names in this book to protect the privacy of our foster children. We will share with you some of our most remembered stories. This book dedicated to all the foster children around the world and to the foster families who decided to take care of them. Again, to protect our foster children their full names are not used. The names are not real to protect them.

FORWORD

I had the pleasure of meeting Aaron and Sandra Stockton in June of 2010. I was a newly licensed Graduate Social Worker who accepted a position with the Board of Child Care Treatment Foster Care (TFC) program.

I at once made a connection with the Stockton's, not only for their love of Pittsburgh, but because they were a very compassionate and caring family. They went beyond to support the children placed in their home, many of whom would call them "Grandma" and "Grandpa." I worked closely with the Stockton's for about 10 years and served countless children together. Each time I placed a child in their family, I was confident that young person would have a safe and nurturing home. There were many times I had to call them and request they accept a youth for a last-minute placement or respite due to extenuating circumstances in the youth's home.

The Stockton's have proved to be flexible and willing to go the extra mile – often driving to pick up the youth or meeting the Case Manager in the middle so that neither party had to drive over an hour. They accepted youth from all over the State of Maryland and recognized the importance of ensuring that young person still had familial connections and could visit approved relatives. To this day, they have youth placed in their home many years ago, that have families of their own, and that still keep a connection with the Stockton's. I am confident that Aaron and Sandra

Stockton made a lasting impact on many of the youth who lived with them, regardless of the length of their stay. I know they have made a lasting impact on me, and I am grateful for the time we worked closely with one another.

Mrs. Kelsey Barlow, LCSW-C

Licensed Certified Social Worker-Clinical

Edinboro University of Pennsylvania - BSW

Catholic University of America - MSW

Let Me Give

*Anonymous author from the book of "Shared
Treasures," compiled by
Roseline J. Young.*

*I do not know how long I will live
But while I live, Lord, let me give
Some comfort to someone in need
By smile or nod – kind word or deed.
And let me do whatever I can
To ease things for my fellow man.
I want naught but to do my part
To lift a tired or weary heart,
To change folks' frowns to smiles again...
Then I will not have lived in vain,
And I will not care how long I will live
If I can give ...and give...and give.*

CHAPTER ONE – FOSTER CARE TERMINOLOGY

Chafee (John H.) Foster Care Independence Act of 1999 Foster Care – The care of a child up to the age of 18 to 21 placed in the care by the foster care system, department of social services by volunteer placement agreement of family, guardian, or court ordered.

Foster Care - Supposed to be a short-term service of a child being placed in a foster family, group facility, or a semi-independent living arrangement.

Emergency Foster Care – Immediate placement of a child due to harm of a child or a family crisis.

Foster Parent – Relative or a Non-relative who is screened and approved by their local department of social services or by a foster care organization to care for, and educate a foster child.

Advocate – As a foster parent you become an advocate for the child placed in your home. Speak for them and get things done for them.

Permanency – A series of court hearings that occur within eleven months of a child entering a home and there after every six months until the child leaves foster care.

Con-Current Permanency – When a backup plan is made for a child's transition out of foster care.

Treatment Foster Care -(TFC) - Training is given to foster parents to care for children with disabilities. The child has an extra caseworker (TFC) that sees them weekly to help them through crisis.

<u>Biological or Birth Parents, adopted parents.</u>

<u>Abandonment, Abuse or Neglect of a child.</u>

<u>Non-Treatment Foster Care</u> – Children with no disabilities

<u>CPS</u> – Child Protective Services. (Appointed through the court system)

<u>CASA or Mentor</u> – Court Appointed Special Advocate or agency appointed for the foster child.

<u>Custody</u> – The legal right and responsibility of either a person or an agency to make decisions about where a child should and could live.

<u>EPSDT</u> – Early Screening, Diagnostic, and Treatment Program. A state program-mandating healthcare that includes full mental, medical, dental, immunizations and laboratory work in screening for medical issues of children placed in the foster care system.

<u>Kinship Placement</u>- A child may transition to a family member's home, other than their parents.

<u>TPR</u> – Termination of Parental Rights. Decided by a Judge.

<u>Home Study</u> – Inspection done at your home to make sure your home is safe for the child to be placed.

<u>Reunification</u> – When a child returns to their home.

<u>Ad Litem</u> – A guardian appointed to act in a lawsuit on behalf of a foster child or other person who is not capable of standing for themselves.

<u>Adoption</u> – Foster parents sometimes decide to adopt. When they become an adoptive parent, they will have all

the rights of the natural parents. In some instances, the adoptive parents will receive a stipend to help with their child until the child becomes 18 years of age.

Guardianship- A process whereby a person other than the biological or adoptive parent assumes the legal responsibility as the foster child's guardian and assumes day-to-day parental responsibilities.

Support Systems – Any organization or persons involved in helping the foster child to have a safe and productive life.

Agency – A public or private organization providing the services for the foster child.

APPLA (Another Planned Permanency Arrangement

Assessments by the foster parent – Weekly logs are required as to the activity of the foster child to include problem behavior and positive behavior. Reports are turned into the agency and sometimes used in court sessions of the Childs permanency plans.

IEP – Individual Education Program – A plan to work with the school system to help the child to adjust and learn without unnecessary barriers.

Independent Living – When a child is moved to an apartment or another program for older children.

Aging Out of Foster Care – "All children — and especially older children in foster care — need and deserve a loving family with no end date. Yet, in the United States, more than 23,000 youth exit foster care and are left to fend for themselves each year." (The Annie E. Casey Foundation)

This scenario — leaving foster care without achieving permanence — carries lifelong consequences. Youth who

age out of foster care face are more likely to engage in
risky behaviors and more likely to experience hardships
such as homelessness, joblessness, early parenthood, and
substance use.

CHAPTER TWO – What Is Foster Care All About.

Foster care is a system of government and non-government agencies, or organizations designed to provide to abandoned, neglected, abused, and trafficked children a placement that is safe, giving them a chance to have a positive life. The system counts on people wanting to serve these children and youths.

Foster care is a powerful way to lift the hopes of the children in the system and show them that there is hope for their futures. The programs recruits foster parents who are kind and loving and can be firm when needed. Being patient, consistent and following through rules and expectations are critical in caring for these victims. The system and the foster parent or parents are the team that will make for a positive outcome in the lives of the children. Remember, "It takes a village to raise a child."

CHAPTER THREE –Getting Started

The very first thing is to be interested. You know someone who was a foster parent or is a foster parent and you have seen a little firsthand. You saw a television commercial or a post on the internet, or an ad in a newspaper. You may have been a foster child and want to give something back to the community. You may just be wondering just why you want to become a foster parent; you just want to know more.

First thing you must do is investigate the diverse types of foster care programs that exist and will best fit you. Respite care (temporary care), relative, kinship care, treatment foster care, elevated needs foster care, medical foster care, unrestrictive foster care, emergency placement and traditional foster care. There are similarities and differences in programs.

Foster parents must be kind, loving, and firm when needed. While a lot of love is a wonderful thing to have, they must also have good parenting and communication skills to be able to reach through to the children. Having parenting skills is immensely helpful for these parents already presenting with parenting skills when they accept a child or youth into their home. Every child is different, and a good parent will be equipped with learning from their experiences and addressing the individual needs of each child or youth in their care.

Therefore, you found a foster care program that you think you want to work with. You attend the foster parent orientation, which not all programs have. You learn all that you may to do, like all the appointments you may have to take your child on. This list includes but is not limited to, eye appointments, dental appointments, mental health therapy appointments, agency meetings, family therapy meetings with the child's family members, teacher parent meetings and more.

Then there are the miscellaneous drives to the movies, a friend's house, and church, outside activities (the recreation centers), after school activities, shopping, to, and from school when the bus does not show up or there is no school bus stop in your neighborhood. You have heard it all and now you are on your way.

1) During your foster care program orientation, you have learned the eleven things you should never say to a foster child or youth placed in your home:

2) What did you do that was so bad that you ended up in foster care?

Not all information is available when you accept the child. Ninety-nine percent of the time, the children are there for no reason of their own.

3) Do not worry you will be home before you know it. Even though the goal is for reunification, it sometimes does not work out that way.

4) Why are you in foster care? This is the same as number two.

5) I understand how you feel. Truly, you do not. No matter what, you cannot step into their shoes and experience what they are feeling.

6) Your mom and dad cannot care about you that much? This is a most horrible one to say. Some parents are incapable of caring for their children because of medical or other reasons. That is different from not caring for them.

7) What is it like to have new parents? You are not their parent. You are a foster parent, and the children are not looking for new parents. Most feel bad about not being home, no matter what their situation was.

8) You must not like your parents very much for letting this happen to you. Most children love their parents very much, no matter what.

9) You are the first foster child that has come to live with us. Your terminology is important, foster child is a label, and most of the children have had enough of labels.

10) It must be horrible being in foster care. Sometimes foster care is a welcomed form of love and security.

11) Changing schools must be hard for you. Sometimes school is a safe place for these children. A place to make new friends and with social media they can stay in touch no matter where they move.

12) You are a foster child. They know that. They do not need reminders.

After your completion of a foster parent orientation, you should have learned that your job is to make the child feel comfortable and accepted in your home. Someday the child may leave, and it will be okay. That, after all is the plan.

<u>CHAPTER 4 - How the Stockton's became involved with the Foster Care System.</u>

It was December 1994 and the empty nest syndrome was upon me. The emptiness was getting to me, but not so much to Aaron. I had just transferred from an active-duty service status to an active reserve military unit. I was sitting at home in the kitchen drinking hot chocolate and reading the Washington Post newspaper. I came across an article that was from a foster care agency called, Alternatives for Youths and Families. The article read boldly, "Looking for foster parents for a teenaged

Caucasian girl that is expecting a child of an afro American boy." It hit me; our house was so empty now with all our children grown up and not living at home any longer. I felt like I had more to give. The enthusiasm and energy that children bring is infectious. I was not ready to live in the quiet house where one could hear a pin drop. I felt the need to be actively parenting. My husband and I had years of experience and met many challenges in our lives as parents. We were more than prepared and we have the flexibility and strength to care for children in our home. I knew that fostering children would go beyond helping the individual child because of the stories my mother told me about her placement in foster care. She made me aware of the fact that we would have to deal with a lot more when taking care of these children.

I felt like I had a loss of purpose. There was no one for us to take care of any longer. We no longer even had a dog. The house was just too quiet. Our job as parents was always for us to teach our children to be able to live independently. I never thought about how it would be when they were no longer at home with us. Therefore, I decided at that moment after reading the story mentioned that I wanted to call that agency and try to get that pregnant teenager to be our foster child. I knew what it felt like being a teen mom. I decided that I should call Aaron to let him know what I was getting ready to do, and not to my surprise he said, "whatever you want Sandra."

I made the call and received an invite for a meeting in person at the agency. When I arrived, there were two other Caucasian women there. They had read the same story and they came for the same reason. We all went to a small conference room and were told that the child we had read about in the Washington Post newspaper was no longer available. I personally felt like that was bait and switch story. The agency needed foster parents and we all showed up and agreed to join the agency. That was December 1994. Orientation started and Aaron had to attend as well. He was not too happy about that but he agreed. During the orientation, we learned that the foster parents must deal with problems of homelessness, substance abuse, child abuse, mental health issues and more. I was thinking to myself, do I want to pursue this? We learned that foster parents give birth parents the chance to receive the required help they need to overcome their problems and get their lives together. Foster parents may also be able to be a role model for the birth parents.

After the training was over, we were more than ready to accept our first child. We knew about a White girl that was in a group home that needed a home; however, they were reluctant to place her with us because we were Black. They said that they had never placed children in homes that were not of their same race. I was feeling some-kind-of-way about that and said, "When will it be time to change that policy?" They decided that since Michelle's mother was in a relationship with a Black man and she had two biracial young brothers it would be okay. So, they agreed. Therefore, in January we welcomed our very first foster child into our home. We were determined to show the agency that a child of any race was welcome in our home and it would work out just fine. Race does not matter. We have always loved a challenge and knew we would do well. Moving forward, that never came up again. We accepted children of all races.

CHAPTER FIVE – Meet Michelle Our First Foster Child

We met Michelle, our first foster daughter in January of 1995 in Charles County, Maryland. Department of Social Services was her funding agency. She was thirteen years old and a very curious teenager. Her hair was deep brown and her eyes were wide and warm. She had some questions for us. She wanted to know if we had any kids at our house and we told her we had adult children who did not live at home. During that first meeting with her and a case manager, we arranged for Michelle to come for a weekend visit the following weekend. We picked her up the following Friday at the agency and she had a large suitcase and a bag of pills for a weekend visit. We signed all the required paperwork to take her for the weekend visit. Upon arrival to our home at 5018 Brimfield Drive, Michelle said to us, "do you live here?" We laughed and Aaron pulled into the driveway. Michelle and I walked up the driveway first while Aaron picked up her suitcase. I went ahead to walk up the stairs and then through the house to our bedroom areas and told her she could select any room that she wanted to sleep in. She chose the one on the street side so she could see in front of the house. We continued with a tour of the house. I guess a five-bedroom house seemed a lot like a mansion compared to the group home where she was living. After the tour, she knew where she was sleeping, where the bathroom was, where the kitchen was, and where our room was.

That night before Michelle went to bed, she shared with me why she wanted to be in a home with no other children, she told me that she had two little brothers and they did not share fathers. She felt as though her mom and her boyfriend were taking advantage of her with care of her two little brothers. I went through her pills and gave her the ones she was to take at bedtime. When we went into our room for the night, I asked Aaron why in the heck they had her on so many medications. I looked them all up in my PDR (physicians' desk reference). She was on medications for depression, anxiety, and mood swings etc. I would find out later that she had been on medications for years. The weekend visit was ending quickly. After Sunday dinner, she and I went to her room to pack up her things. I was sitting on the bed and she came and sat down beside me. She wanted to stay but that was not allowed. I told her that we would ask if the move from the group home to our house could happen soon. A week later Michelle, was living with us.

We now had a ninth grader living with us. It was exciting to have this child in our home. No more empty nest syndrome for us. We were terribly busy the first month or so, registering her for school at Douglas Senior High School, making doctor appointments, dental appointments and therapy appointments for her. I asked Michelle about the medications and when was the last time she saw the doctor who prescribed the medications. She told them that she only saw the doctor once a year and he always ask her if she is okay and then renews her medications. I was just looking at her and thinking to myself, hell no, that is not going to be the practice while she is with us. Seeing the psychiatrist was the first appointment I made for her, then the therapist.

We had to take her shopping for school clothes, using our own funds because a stipend for her would not come until thirty days later. That is how foster care programs work, almost everywhere. Sometimes the agencies reimburse and sometimes they do not, it depends on their budget. We were financially stable and had no worries. Michelle asked us not to tell people she was our foster child because White kids can have Black parents. We told her that we had to tell people in the school system that she was a foster child for they would surely know when we registered her, but we will not share that with everyone. She asked to call us mom and dad and we said it would work for us. This was all new to us. That day we decided that moving forward we would ask children what they wanted to call us. We gave them choices of Mr. Stockton, Miss Sandi, mom, dad, Grandmom, granddad, aunt, and uncle, whatever they decided we would accept because they had to find their own comfortability.

About two weeks in we developed a chart for her chores, explained to her how she would earn allowance, and earn extra money for special projects. We allowed her to write down the house rules that she wanted. We went over them together and met her halfway. Michelle settled in quickly, making new friends at school and in the neighborhood. We developed a nice family atmosphere for all three of us. She would soon meet our baby girl, Karmentrina who just dropped by to see me. My daughters often dropped by without notice. They both had door keys to our house. When Karmentrina walked in she encountered Michelle and she said hello to her. Michelle responded to her, "hello" Karmentrina was giving me the strangest look and said and who is Michelle mom? I responded; "she is your foster sister." News travels fast, our daughter Kimmy Jo came to visit us very soon after Karmentrinas visit and met Michelle. Our sons would meet her later for they did not live in town. Before long, my entire family knew that Aaron and I had a foster child. Michelle met so many of them in the first few months. Everyone just loved her.

One day when Aaron and I were away from home, Karmentrina stopped by to visit. Michelle was home with Aaron's mother, whom had come to visit with us for a week. We returned home later that evening. Karmentrina and Michelle had a little confrontation. Per Karmentrinas words, she came by to cut coupons out of the Sunday Washington Post. She told me that Michelle snatched the paper from her and told her she could not stop by and do whatever she wanted to do because she did not live here. Karmentrina was so angry and told me that it was lucky for Michelle that her Grandmom stepped between them because she was about to teach Michelle a lesson for pushing her and snatching the paper from her. I told her I was glad as well and told Karmentrina that she could not do harm to our foster child for we would be in big trouble. I did not count on, sibling rivalry between my foster child and my biological child that was one problem that I did not think out. Just how was I going to get Michelle to understand the difference? That evening I went to Michelle's room and had a talk with her about Karmentrina and Kimmy Jo. I told her that they both had keys and could come and go as they wish for, I have always allowed them to do that. After a few tears and a saddened face, she came and sat down beside me and said she understood. I told her that it would be nice if she told Karmentrina that she was sorry the next time she saw her and she did. After talking with her and Karmentrina, things smoothed over and there were never any other issues. Michelle always wanted to spend the day at Karmentrina's house.

We introduced her to many things in our culture and she introduced us to country music. One day after school, she came into the house all excited to tell me that Garth Brooks and Faith Hill were going to be at a concert in Virginia. I was like who is he? She responded; "Mom he is the greatest, can I please go for my birthday?" I told her that I would check with dad (she was calling us mom and dad by now) when he came home after work and let her know in the morning. I discussed the concert with Aaron that evening before bedtime. He looked at me and said, "Who is Garth Brooks?" I told him a country singer that Michelle loves. He told me that I should take her because it could be a mother, daughter-bonding event. I told him, "Don't even try that!" We decided to flip a coin for it, I chose heads, and he chose tails. I won the flip. Therefore, the next morning before Michelle left for school, I told her that dad would be going with her. She was so happy and said; "I have never been to a concert before." Later that morning I bought the two tickets for the concert and they both attended. Aaron looked through his closet and found his cowboy boots, duster jacket, and his Stetson hat that he had from when we were stationed in New Mexico. He was all set and hyped.

They both returned home after the concert and Michelle was so hyped. Aaron on the other hand looked beat. Michelle went on to say that Aaron fell asleep and was snoring most of the concert. Michelle said she was so happy that the concert noise was so loud that no one probably paid any attention to Aaron snoring. In Aaron's defense, he said he woke up when Faith Hill was performing. Michelle listened to all country stations; we became accustomed and play country music to this day.

Spring of 1995 was upon us and all was going well, until Michelle came home from school crying and telling me that she had a dreadful day in school. I went ahead to ask her what had happened and she told me that a few White girls in her class called her a "nigger lover" because she hung around with Black girls in her class. I sat down beside her in the kitchen, told her that there would be people like that in the world, and told her to keep her head up high. I asked her if she wanted Aaron and me to go to the school with her to work it out and she said no, "I will be okay!" I told her to let me know if anyone touches her or tries to harm her in any way, because things would certainly be worked out.

Summer 1995, Michelle, and I went with my two daughters to look at wedding dresses for Karmentrina, our baby girl. We were walking on the crowded streets of Georgetown, Washington, DC. A small crowd was staring at us and I told the girls to ignore them and to keep walking. However, Michelle did not get the memo, she looked at them and yelled, "what are you looking at, you never saw a Black family with a While child?" That surprised me, I knew then that she was an outspoken person and I did not have to worry about her speaking up for herself.

<u>CHAPTER SIX – Meet Sherry Our Second Foster Daughter</u>

It was about seven months in when we received a call to take an emergency placement for a twelve-year-old Caucasian girl who was in the system. Her two younger brothers accused her of inappropriately touching them. Department of Social Services was her funding agency. Sherry lived with her father and two younger brothers. Their mother was incarcerated. The placement was to be for about four and a half weeks or less. Michelle was not feeling that, remember she wanted no other children to be in our house except her. I explained to Michelle that it was just a temporary situation and she did not have to share her bedroom. I told her that she could help me out with her because she was so young. She liked that idea and it did not take long for her to intervene with helping me. It was summer and Sherry arrived with her caseworker early in the morning. She was short and full figured for a little girl of twelve years of age. I introduced myself to both of them and then called Michelle in to meet both of them. The caseworker left soon afterwards. Aaron would meet Sherry when he returned home from work. That afternoon Sherry walked into the kitchen where Michelle and I were sitting at the kitchen counter watching television. She was looking like a little woman, make-up, bright red lipstick, and nail polish. Michelle looked at me as if to say, "Are you going to say something?" I was surprised and commented to Sherry that I thought the makeup was not a good color for her. She just looked at me and said; "my daddy bought it for me." I told her that she, Michelle, and I would go to the store the next day and buy something that complemented her complexion.

The next day I kept my word, she came home with pink lipstick, and clear nail polish, like Michelle had. I told her that she could now look like a twelve year old and to wait until she was older for the bright red colors. We would soon meet Sherry's father for he had visitation rights. However, she was not to be around the boys alone. Although she was only going to be with us for a brief period, we decided to give her an allowance because Michelle was getting an allowance. About three weeks in Sherry told me that her father was going to take her and her two brothers to the movies. I thought that was nice, at least all of them would be together. Sherry's father dropped her off about five hours later and I was surprised when Sherry told me that just she and her father went to the movies alone and that she used her allowance to pay for them both. I asked her why her father did not pay and she responded, "He said he did not have any money." I was not feeling that, but it is what it was. The investigation was soon over and Sherry returned home to her father and two brothers. The accusations were unfounded. Apparently, the older brother lied to his teacher to get Sherry into trouble. Summer was now ending and school would start soon.

CHAPTER SEVEN Meet Nickema Our Third Foster Daughter

That call came for us to consider accepting another child who was in a detention center, at Boys Village where they were accepting boys and girls at that time. After hearing about her story, we decided to accept her. Department of Juvenile Justice was her funding agency. She attended an alternative school, Croom High School in Upper Marlboro, Maryland. No big deal, we took care of getting her registered. Nickema was a sixteen-year-old Black girl who was in the tenth grade. It was now 1996. I told Michelle right away when she came home from school that Nickema was coming and to my surprise, she was okay with that. She just looked at me and said; "mom we have more than enough room." I smiled; we sure do. We met Nickema when they dropped her off at our house a few days later. It was time to repeat our routine of, meet, greet, and orient Nickema to our home as well as to our family. I had Michelle orient Nickema to the house and the house rules. The girls got along okay. Although Nickema was not very talkative, we all got along together. We introduced Nickema to our two daughters shortly after her arrival. It was important for our girls to know our foster children for we depended on them to look after them in a pinch. We never sent our children to another foster home for respite because we want them to feel like family, not visitors. Nickema was my "whistler in dark child," a quiet child who had barely nothing to talk about with anyone of us. She had a beautiful smile and did respond non-verbally. She used extraordinarily little words, but always pleasant.

One evening after school, I went into her room to ask how school was going. Her response, okay! I decided I would probe a little to find out her back-story and to my surprise, she did share. She told me that she lived with her mom, two brothers, and her mom's boyfriend. She said her mom was very mean to her, always calling her "no good bitch" and telling her she was "ugly." Nickema was far from ugly. I asked her how she ended up in Boys Village and she shared that story as well. She said she went to a party with her mom's permission and she had a curfew time, but stayed at the party a little too late and knew she could not make it home on time. Therefore, she chose to ask two boys who had a car for a ride home. Apparently,

the police stopped the car. The car was reported stolen.
They were all three arrested and ended up in Boys Village.
Nickema's mom decided that she did not want her to return
home. Therefore, she ended up in the system at our home.
Nickema never really told us or anyone else any more of
her family or personal issues. It did not matter to us
because now she was safe, happy, and protected. We were
happy that we could provide a safe environment for her.
She too was in therapy and on multiple medications. I was
taking Nickema to mental health therapy for almost eight
months when the therapist called me into her office in front
of Nickema and told me that Nickema never talked to her.
She just sits there and waits for forty-five minutes to go by.
I told the therapist that I would talk with her caseworker at
the agency and get back to her as soon as possible. I could
not believe that the therapist took that damn long to share
that information with me.

In the mean time we received a call from the agency that
they were moving Michelle to a step-down program for she
no longer qualified for treatment foster care. She was no
longer on any medication and having no mental health
therapy. I could not believe it. I called Aaron at work to let
him know and he said; "well babe, you know the plan is for
the kids to leave, you knew it would not be permanent." I
was emotionally broken about the fact that the agency was
moving her. I pleaded with them to keep her in place, but
they said they could not justify it. I had to tell Michelle; I
did not want her to hear it from the case manager first.
Aaron and I told her together. She started to cry; she was
so angry and ran out of our room to her bedroom. I waited
for about a half hour to go into her room. Her face was so
red from crying. I told her that we would visit her and that
she could come to visit us as well. Michelle would be

leaving us in a few weeks. I told the whole family so everyone could say good-bye to her before she left. Michelle had accumulated so many things since she had been living with us. Aaron bought boxes for us to pack her things. Michelle was going to a White family who had two Black boys under the age of ten that they were adopting. We did not feel good about that. It sounded like the environment she came to us from. Michelle would leave us soon.

It would not be long before I started getting calls from the first foster family where Michelle was placed. They told me that she was acting out terribly. I asked them just what did she do that was so terrible and the foster mom gave me an ear full. I just listened intensely to her. She told me that at her home at dinnertime, they all go around the table and each one says something that they are grateful for that day. She said that when it was Michelle's turn, she said; "I am not grateful to be anyone's slave and do not like picking up after your kids." I told her that was a very new thing for Michelle for at our house we just took turns saying grave only. I asked to visit Michelle and she invited Aaron and me. We did go to see Michelle a few days later and took her out for a ride and we talked at length. We heard Michelle's version of what was going on. It seems that since she was the oldest, she had to do many more chores and Michelle told us that she was not having that. We told her that we would check with the agency to see if we could get her for two weekends a month and she seemed okay with that. It was not a week later, when Michelle called me about nine o'clock in the evening to tell me that she ran away. I asked her where she was and she refused to tell me because she thought I would call the police. I promised her that I would not do that. She was living about an hour from us; I was worried about her being out at night alone in McDonalds, where she said she was. I asked her for the address so I could come to pick her up, but I did not keep that promise. I called the agency on call person and told them where she was and they sent someone to pick her up. She was so mad at me. I would find out the next day that she was moved to another family. Things did not go so well and Michelle ended up back with us later on.

I finally spoke with the caseworker of our foster care program about Nickema not taking part in therapy and they told me they would talk with her paying agency, Department of Social Services. The house was so different with Michelle gone, I was depressed about that for a while, but knew I had no choice. Nickema gave us no problems, no school issues, or home issues. She was making A's, B's, and C's., she told us she never had passing grades in any school she ever attended. We were surprised. I guess she did take part in school. Just as quiet as a church mouse with us and her therapist. She loved being around our girls and that was good for her. She especially loved being around our baby girl Karmentrina. That was an asset for Aaron and me. We knew then she would talk.

I came home from work one evening and Nickema was sitting at the kitchen counter eating some snacks. I spoke and she spoke back. I noticed that she was wearing one of my sweaters. Therefore, I asked her where did she get it from and she responded; "I took it from your closet." I told her that she did not have permission and she responded; "I did not think you would mind because you have many sweaters." I said to her that it was not okay and that she should ask the next time she wanted to wear something that belonged to me. That evening when Aaron came home from work, I told him about the incident and that I needed him to buy a lock for our bedroom door, no sooner said, it was done that evening. Aaron went to Home Depot and purchased a lock for our bedroom door. I would make sure that she asked the next time. (After talking with Nickema on November 16, 2021, we laughed about that incident.) The agency decided to have team meetings to discuss a new placement for Nickema. Nickema would leave us soon because I was hoping, as the team was that she would do better with another family. She was moved with another Black family and was there for a noticeably brief time. Nickema would tell us that they did nothing for her and that they were in it for the money, she did not get an allowance as she did when she was with us. Therefore, she was placed again with a White family (we broke the color barrier) where she did quite well and graduated with them. She aged out and moved to independent living. Nickema told me that her mother reached out to her when she aged out. They went out to dinner and hung out. She said her mother also signed for her first car; she was shocked by all of it. She would soon find out that her mother had breast cancer and she would die soon from breast cancer. I told Nickema that her mother might have been making peace with her. We do not know what her mother may have gone through when she was a child. At twenty-one Nickema found herself in a relationship and became pregnant with her first and only child, a son. Things did not work out for the relationship, so Nickema decided to leave the relationship... She would contact me about twenty years ago, crying and telling me that her son was taken from her and she needed help to get him back. I listened to her story and told her to stop crying and listen. When she calmed down, I told her that I would have Karmentrina call her to help her work things out. Karmentrina was now living in Virginia, as was Nickema. Karmentrina was an activist for safety of children and she worked for Fairfax County Government. Karmentrina would reach out to Nickema and help her, as I knew she would. Nickema was at a metro station and spanked her son for something and some White woman decided to call the police on her for child abuse. They took her son. Karmentrina went to bat for Nickema and went to court with her until she was given custody back of her son. Karmentrina also was able to get her son into the Fairfax County head start program. Nickema was on her way now. Her son is now 22 years of age and she is a single independent woman doing well. We are immensely proud of Nickema.

I am glad that she remembered that I was a registered nurse. She reached out to me on social media because she had major surgery and wanted some advice. I was grateful that I responded to her. She remembered that she had a lifeline with us if she ever needed us. We are connected and communicate as if it was just yesterday when she left our home. We hope to visit her soon for she is no longer in the state of Maryland where we live.

As for Michelle, she reached out to me on social media about four years ago she messaged me and ask if I was the Sandra Stockton who had a husband named Aaron Stockton and I responded that I was indeed that person and ask her who she was because she had a name I did not recognize. She responded back; I am Michelle, your foster daughter." I was so excited to hear from her. She told me that she was stationed in Germany with her army husband and three daughters. That made me smile because she said she would always marry a military man like Aaron. She told me that

when she returns to stateside to visit her mother in
Maryland, she would stop by to see us and she did.
Moreover, we had a conversation about her mother whom
she had just visited before she got to me. She just looked at
me, and said, Mama you were right, some people never
change. My mom will never change. We have been
communicating ever since she contacted me four years ago,
Michelle is an independent woman holding her own and
has three beautiful daughters the youngest are a set of
twins. We hope to visit her again in the future, for she lives
many states away from us.

CHAPTER EIGHT Meet SHARON Our Fourth Foster Daughter

It was May of 1996 when Aaron received a page from
the agency. He phoned me to call them to see what they
wanted because he was busy at work. I made the call to the
agency; they had an emergency placement that they wanted
us to consider taking. They told me her name was Sharon
and that she was a Black twelve-year-old. That was young.
I told them I would get back to them. I called Aaron to
discuss it and he wanted to know if I thought I could deal
with a twelve-year-old. I told him that it was a temporary
placement and that I thought we could do it for a brief
period. Brian a case manager at that time drove her to our
house and gave us some history. Department of Social
Services was her funding agency. Sharon was so cute, she
had red hair and light brown eyes, and she was so delightful
looking. Placed with another foster parent, Miss Hilda of
our agency but she could not deal with Sharon's tantrums.

Apparently, she had been adopted by an elderly couple as a little girl. We were told that the father passed and soon after his passing, Sharon began to act out, getting in trouble in school, lying, and having tantrums. Therefore, she was removed from her home by request of her adoptive mother. We were told that the agency wanted to keep her in her home school until the end of the school year, so that meant we had to provide transportation for her to and from school, about twenty-two miles from us because Department of Social Services and our agency had no one to provide the transportation for her to and from her home school. We agreed and were paid mileage. That was for May and June until the school year ended. Our whole family all soon met Sharon and they just loved the little brat.

One summer afternoon when school was out, our grandson Keen came to stay with us for the summer, he was about her age. He found out that Sharon was afraid in the dark by accident. She was upstairs in her room one evening and Keej turned off the hall light when he left his room that was across from hers. She opened her door to a dark hallway and started screaming, Miss Sandi, Keej turned off the light. We did not know she was afraid of the dark because before Keej came she always kept the hall light on. Every now and then, Keej would threaten to turn off the light and I had to scold him about that.

One Saturday afternoon Sharon had a fit about something. I said no to her about something. For the life of me, I cannot remember what it was, but I do remember that she said she was going to kill herself. She ran to her room and I followed. Aaron was out in front of the house washing his car. Sharon ran over to the window and stuck her leg out of the window as if she was going to jump. I decided I would help her. I ran over to her and started yelling, "You want to jump, and you want to jump, let me help you. I grabbed her around the waist and was pushing her through the window (I firmly had my grip around her waist). She than put both of her feet on the outer rim of the window and started yelling; "Mr. Ace your wife is crazy, she is trying to kill me." I was yelling: I am just trying to help her kill herself." The neighbors across the street were looking at us by now and Aaron said to them; "do not worry they do that all the time. We had such a laugh that night.

It would not be long before we experienced the full-blown tantrums when she did not get her way. She started taking things that did not belong to her and when I wanted the things back, she would act out. One time she went into my home office and started picking up, throwing things of mine, and breaking them. I just looked at her and was wondering, "Why in the heck did I agree to take this little girl with the history of tantrums." I just continued to remain quiet and just kept looking at her until she stopped. She just looked at me shaking her head and crying. I finally asked her if she was done. Sharon did not respond. I left my office and started up the stairs to her room. Nickema was not back from school yet. I started picking up her things, throwing them, and stomping them into the floor, she was yelling; "stop it Miss Sandi, Stop it." I walked out of her room and she yelled; "I am going to tell Mr. Ace on you."

I at once called the agency and told them what had happened. I told them not to worry about her things for we would replace them. The case manager thought that they should make a visit to discuss this and they sent someone the next evening. Brian, the case manager whom I knew well came. I told him that I was going to deny everything she said during the visit. I wanted to teach her another lesson as well, about lying on people. The meeting went as planned. Everything that she told Brian I denied and said that Sharon was lying on me. At one point she looked at me and said; "I can't believe that you are sitting there lying to Brian, you are a grownup." I knew then I was getting to her. The case manager soon closed out the meeting and told Sharon that she was going to have to stop her lying if she ever wanted anyone to believe her. Nickema was gone soon and that left plenty of time for us to work with Sharon.

One evening we were sitting in the back yard barbecuing and Sharon and I had a long talk. I asked her why she was always lying and having tantrums, which started soon after her adopted father passed. She said to me that she wanted to go to her father's funeral and her adoptive mother decided that she was too young to attend. She also told Aaron and me that all she wanted was to visit her father's gravesite. That night Aaron and I decided to make it happen, a visit to her father's gravesite. That was relatively easy. Sharon had the obituary. We read and found out where he was buried and with permission, we took her to visit her father's gravesite. Soon after that visit, she was a changed child and was back in her home by the start of the new school year. About eight years ago, Aaron ran into Sharon at McKay's grocery store. She apparently spotted him and called out to him. Aaron said she was her bubbly self. She told him that she was single, and had six children and that she took care of all of them. We pray for many blessings for her and her children.

CHAPTER NINE - Meet Maria Our Fifth Foster Daughter

The house was empty again and a new request came in for a placement for a Hispanic eighteen-year-old young woman who was in the independent living program. She was from a broken home and lived with her mother. Department of Social Services was her funding agency. This was our first independent living foster child. Maria was a high school dropout and was in the program because she was acting out at home and she had a history of being a run-a-way. We were not too sure about that but we needed the experience with independent living children, because it did not come with a playbook. It was the end of August 1997. We started having issues soon after she came to live with us. About two weeks in, we went on a trip, her, and me to Karmentrina's house in Alexandria, Virginia. After our arrival, she started asking me to go and buy her some cigarettes. Well that was not going to happen. She threatened me and said; "If you do not get me some cigarettes, I am going to leave and find a cigarette. I said; "Do what you must missy because I will not be buying you any cigarettes." About twenty minutes later, I went outside and Maria was not on the front porch. She was gone.

I immediately called the Alexandria Police Department to report her missing and when I told them, she was eighteen they refused to send anyone out to talk with me. I then told them that she was a foster child and by policy of the agency, I had to report her missing and get a police report. A young Hispanic officer showed up and I explained everything to him, He wrote up a missing person report for me and gave it to me. Before he left, he asked me; "why do you take care of these delinquent kids?" I responded that someone has too. Maria was missing for about three days and finally showed up in front of the house in Upper Marlboro, Maryland with a Black male who said he just gave her a lift home. While I was talking with him, Aaron came out and took a picture of his license plate just in case we needed it. He got nervous and said I did not know she was a run-a-way. You do not have to worry about me coming here to pick her up. However, she was old enough to be in that car if she chose to be. That was a big red flag for us. Worrying about her for those three days was too stressful for me. It did not seem to bother Aaron; he took that in stride because she was eighteen. When she ran away for the second time, we decided to put our thirty-day notice in to have her removed from our home. The agency understood and after she left, we never heard from her again and that was okay.

CHAPTER TEN - Meet Jennifer Our Six Foster Daughter

Jennifer was a Black eighteen-year-old young lady. Department of Social Services was her funding agency. Her placement was an emergency placement, to be with us for about two weeks. Well, that was about the time she ran away and convinced Michelle, who was back with us temporarily, to run with her. Michelle was placed back with us as an emergency placement between assigned foster parents. They were back in a day or so later and both removed from our home. I felt like I needed a break. So, we told the agency we were taking a respite for thirty days and we did.

<u>CHAPTER ELEVEN - Meet Jackie and Lynn, our Seventh and Eighth Foster Daughters</u>

They were admitted to our home within days of each other. Both were Black and both 17 years of age. The Department of Social Services was their funding agency. They were both living with a single parent, their mothers. They would both be attending Douglas Senior High School. The principals and guidance counselors knew us quite well now. Registering them was a breeze. They were both coming from group homes. This was a time when the state was trying to get children out of group home environments. They were both in the tenths grade. They got along very well and shared a room in our home. They worked out the dish schedule and handled keeping their room tidy. Jackie was in the system because she wanted to be more grownup than she was. Hanging around older boys over twenty-one years of age. She always lied about her age. I heard her on the phone one day talking to a man and she was telling him that she was thirty. I waited until she was off the phone and asked her why she was in such a hurry to be an old woman. She looked at me and laughed. I had Kimmy Jo to talk with her about that. She told me her boyfriend was twenty. She was seventeen, no big deal really, she said. However, the agency and her mom were against it. So, we did not allow him to visit her at our house. Jackie did very well with us. She was smart and funny. She told me that her boyfriend was White and I asked her if she had a picture and she showed it to me. He was not White but light enough to pass. She would do well and leave us in about a year. She contacted me by phone when she aged out. She was now living with that boyfriend and they had an adorable son. She invited Aaron and me to visit them and we did. It was a pleasant encounter. At that point, we thought Jackie was going to do just fine.

Lynn on the other hand was having many problems in school, quite a few suspensions for leaving out of class without permission and being kicked off the school bus for inappropriate behavior. Inappropriate behavior in school with boys. Lynn was so angry with me one summer evening because I would not allow her to go with a young man who showed up in his car to pick her up. I called Aaron out of the house who told the young man that he was too old to see Lynn. He told him not to come to our home again for any young girl living in our house. I pulled out my polaroid camera and snapped a picture of his car. He was repeatedly saying he was sorry and that he would not return. He never did. Well, that night Lynn had a treat for us, a tantrum like we never knew she would do. She walked out of the house, saying; "Miss Sandi you are going to be sorry." I responded back to her, "I don't think so. "She continued and stopped in front of the driveway, in the street, and said she was not going to move and was going to lay there until a car ran her over and killed her. I tried to convince her to get up. She just put her hands over her ears as if she could not hear me and would not get up. Aaron was standing in the doorway calling out to me to come in the house. So, I did. After about 15 minutes, she was still laying on our hot ground with her hands over ears.

Therefore, I decided to call the Prince Georges County Police Department (PG) and told them my situation. Surely after I made that phone call, two young PG county police officers showed up. They talked to her for some time to convince her to get up and she just would not do it. Therefore, one of the officers said to her, "you can stay lying in the street in front of the driveway all you want too but you are moving out of the street, or you are going to jail." Lynn decided that jail was not an option. She laid there in the driveway until the wee hours of the evening, and finally came into the house and apologized and asks for dinner, as if the whole event never happened.

One Saturday morning I was in my basement office and I heard a very loud crash above my head. Aaron was not at home at that time. I ran upstairs to Lynn's room and she was lying on the floor with her eyes rolled back. I checked her pulse and it was faint. I turned her on her side and propped her. It was difficult for me because she was over 250 pounds. I ran to the kitchen to call 911. They were there in record time. They struggled to get her out of the room and down the stairs, then outside down the outside porch stairs to the ambulance. Lynn had swallowed pills. I followed in my car to Southern Maryland Hospital. They admitted her to the psychiatric ward. I could not tell them what she swallowed because I kept all medications locked in my room, a practice we did for all the children that were on medications of any kind. I finally had time to call the agency and a case manager came to meet me. They contacted her biological mother. When she showed up, she and I talked a long time while they were working with Lynn. She told me that Lynn was bipolar and tried to commit suicide several times and one time she jumped out of a second story window to kill herself. The agency never told us that she had a suicidal history.

We went to visit her every evening while she was an inpatient. At one visit, she told us that she did that often to get a vacation in the hospital. She was bizarre. A behavior that we had not seen from her. Karmentrina gave us breaks and she went to visit sometimes. Aaron and I decided that we were not comfortable taking her back. She returned to us briefly then later placed in an alternative placement. Her mother phoned me a few weeks later to thank us for taking care of Lynn. I thought that was very thoughtful.

It would be two years later when I received a telephone message on my home phone. It was from a school invited Aaron and me to Lynn's high school graduation. They left a number and I returned the call the next day. A woman answered and identified herself with the school name. I told her about the call and she said; "Lynn wanted to invite you and your husband to her high school graduation." I responded, Lynn.... She said yes and gave me the date and time of her graduation. I could not wait to give that information to Aaron. We did indeed go to her high school graduation, and we just could not believe it. I never thought she would ever make it out of school. When we arrived at the school, her mother was there with her other children. I was so excited to see her and the children I just could not believe that Lynn was graduating. So, the ceremony was soon starting and we all had to take our seats. In addition, Lynn was the spokesperson and she sang for the opening. After she was finished singing and speaking. She pointed to Aaron and me in the audience and asked us to stand up. I was thinking oh Lord; I am not even dressed for this. We stood up and she said to the whole audience these are my foster parents it is because of them why I am graduating today she looked at us and said, "I love you guys' Miss Sandi and Mr. Ace thank you so much." We were so proud of her. She was really listening to us, even when we thought she was not. What a blessing for her to graduate after such a rocky road in her young life. We would never hear from Lynn again.

CHAPTER TWELVE - Game Changer

We received a request to accept two boys into our home whom were presently in a group home. We never thought much about that, however, there was an incident presented at one of our monthly foster parent meetings. A foster girl accused her foster father of inappropriate behavior. It would soon be unfounded; however, such an investigation is stressful to go though. I did not want that to happen to us, so I told Aaron that I thought it was a clever idea to start fostering boys because he was home more often than I was. Another reason was that we had grandsons that came around often that they could friend. That would be good for the foster children.

A John Hopkins University study of a group of foster children in Maryland found that children in foster care are four times more likely to be sexually abused than their peers not in this setting, and children in-group homes are

28 times more likely to be abused. It is a fact that there are horrible foster parents out there. The foster care system on paper is a picture-perfect system. There is a shortage of foster parents, shortage of funding, not enough qualified case managers, who are to help with appointments, etc., which causes the foster parents to do so much more with no compensation for the extras. Many foster parents just give up. This causes the system to place children in-group homes, extended stays in detention, etc. We chose to help. If we could care for these two boys and get them out of the group home that would not fix the broken the system issues, but it could help a little.

<u>CHAPTER THIRTEEN - Meet Jaquan, Richard, and Charlie</u>

Richard and Jaquan would arrive within two days of each other. Jaquan was Black and Richard was White. Department of Social Services was the funding agency for Richard. The Department of Juvenile Justice was Jaquan's funding agency. They did not know each other prior to their arrival. Both boys were eighteen years of age but Jaquan was a few months older than Richard was. They were in the independent living program, which was new to us. A program designed for providing services for education, employment, housing, and budgeting to support or aid a youth with transition from teenager to adulthood period. Our routine would be a little different moving forward. Jaquan was in the group home because he was living with his aunt and his cousin. One day his aunt found a gun under her sofa cushion and she blamed it on Jaquan. Jaquan swore to the authorities that it belonged to his cousin, her son. Jaquan sent there to live with his mom's sister because she was worried about him involvement with the gangs. His father was a lifer and his mom thought he would do better living in Maryland. Richard, removed from his home because he was living with his mother who was an alcoholic, and so was Richard. Both boys had clothing on their arrival. Aaron oriented them to our home. They both chose the bedroom that they wanted. They were given clean linen, towels, face cloths and a clothe hamper. Aaron took them shopping for personal items and got them settled in their own rooms.

I would have a conversation with the boys that evening to find out if they could do dishes, cook, cut grass, and such. They both said they could cook eggs and bacon and that was a start. Jaquan saw that we had a dishwasher and said; "we used the dishwasher at my aunt's house." I took that opportunity to tell the boys that we did not use the dishwasher in our house unless it was a holiday and there were many dishes to clean. Richard wanted to know why? I told them both that when they were ready to transition to independent living, they needed to know how to wash dishes because they may not have a dishwasher when they transitioned out of our house. They were going to learn how to clean house and do their own laundry while they were with us and how to manage their money.

They would be registering for a GED program and find part time jobs. Richard would have to attend a program for alcohol addiction (Alcoholics Anonymous, AA). Jaquan had to take anger management classes. Aaron took Richard to the first AA meeting and they were both joking when they returned home. Richard said he stood up and said; "My name is Richard and I am an alcoholic. He said Aaron got up and said; "My name is Aaron and I am not an alcoholic. I am here with my son." Richard had a driver's license and knew how to drive. Jaquan did not have a driver's license, but he told us he knew how to drive. They were both smokers and I did not plan to try to make them stop. There were other issues that needed worked on, that were the plan. Jaquan and Richard got along well and we just loved them. We had no issues; they felt like our grands they called us Miss Sandi and Mr. Ace. They got along good with our grands even though they were a little older than our grands were. Jaquan would find a day job at Wendy's rather quickly. We supplied transportation for the first few weeks than taught him how to ride the bus. Richard found a part time job at Subway sandwich shop in Upper Marlboro about ten minutes from our house, so transportation was easier on us. Karmentrina volunteered to pick up Richard sometimes and I found out later she had the hookup for chocolate chip cookies. Aaron allowed Richard to work with him sometimes to help him to earn more money because he wanted to save for a car. Aaron had a small contract with Farmers Bank of Virginia doing miscellaneous things. Although both boys made money working, we saved money monthly for them as well, to make sure they would have money when they left our home. Every child that came through our home left with money. Our agency also saved $50.00 each month for the children. They received that money as well when they transitioned out.

Both boys received counseling from their counselors weekly. They were not in mental health therapy. They were getting amazingly comfortable; I had no reason not to trust things around them. Mistake! One chilly winter Saturday morning, Richard decided that he needed to buy a pack of cigarettes. Mr. Ace was not at home, so, he took Mr. Ace's Ford pickup keys without my permission. If Mr. Ace had been home, he would have taken him to get cigarettes. I did not know why he just did not ask me to take him. I was in my room watching television and did not hear the truck leave. He could have gotten away with it; however, the truck ran out of gas when he was on his way back. He came down to my room and asked if he could talk to me. His face was so red. I asked; "were you outside, your face is so red?" He goes on to say; "about that, I took Mr. Aces' truck to go and buy a pack of cigarettes." That got my attention! I said, "What, did you wreck it?" He said, "No, I drifted it into a parking space on the side of the road on Roblee Drive. I called Aaron and told him what happened. He was not to upset and said, "I guess we will be locking up all car keys from now on." Had we told the agency, they would have moved him and authored a report. At the end of the day, our son Kevin took his dads car without my knowing it while he was stationed in South Korea. I did not realize the car had been driven until about a week later. I just so happened to take a scenic route home, drove from the top of our street, and noticed that the truck had been wrecked. I was in a panic because I knew my husband was to return from overseas in thirty days. I gave Richard a pass because he was honest with me. He was that kid that you could love on contact.

About eight months in the agency contacted us to see if we would take a temporary placement of a fifteen-year-old White boy who was in ninth grade. I was someone concerned because I did not want the older boys influencing him, but after much thought with Aaron we decided to accept Charlie. It was about April, and we had planned a trip to Disney and decided that we would take him along if he were still living with us when the time came to travel to Florida. Charlies' issues were stealing, obesity, smoking marijuana and running away from home. He ran away many times until the court system decided he would be better off living in a controlled environment. He was on a list for placement, and they hoped it would not be too long before he was placed. Therefore, we accepted him. We did not want it to be permanent because of his history of being a run-a-way child. We registered him for school and bought all the supplies that he needed.

Richard and Jaquan saved a lot of money for their upcoming trip to Florida, which they had in their rooms. I told them of Charlie's history of taking things, so they would be careful where they laid their money. They both decided that they were going to set a trap for Charlie unknown to Aaron and me, to find out if they could trust him. They planted twenty dollars in the recreation room, a place where Charlie had to search to find it. That evening when Jaquan and Richard came home from work, they cornered Charlie to let him know that they knew he stole their money. I heard them in Charlie's room, and I did not interfere. Charlie ended up crying and confessing. I entered the room to pretend that I did not know what was going on. Therefore, they told me what happened. I told Charlie he was going to have to pay the twenty dollars back to the boy out of his ten dollar a week allowance that he was receiving form us. He paid them back in four weeks at five dollars a week. They all got along from that day on and there were no more stealing issues in the house that we were aware of. The school year was winding down for

Charlie. It was late May, and I received a call from Douglas High School from the principal. He said, "Mrs. Stockton we cannot find your son, Charlie. He was signed in this morning at attendance but now at third period he is unaccounted for." I told him that I was on my way to the school and was there within thirty minutes, worried silly. When I arrived at the school and entered the office, my son Charlie was sitting there smelling like marijuana, all flushed, and looking scared. I just looked at him and said nothing. The principle came out of his office and called me in to talk with him. In my brain, I was trying to come up with how I was going to get the principle not to suspend this child. To make a long story short, Charlie was given in school suspension for the rest of the school year, which was only about three weeks. Now we must put him into a drug program.

It was getting close to vacation time, and everyone was excited for none of them had ever been to Disney World in Florida. I came home from work, Aaron was waiting on the front porch for me, and I knew something was going on. He told me that Richard said he spent all his money to buy a pound of marijuana. That did not make sense to me because he had not been smoking. We went to his room and Aaron asked Richard where the Marijuana was, and he did not answer. We did not press him but when we walked into the kitchen where Jaquan and Charlie were sitting eating snacks; Jaquan told us that he gave his money to his mom for her rent. I went back to Richards's room alone and told him that Jaquan told me what had happened. I asked how his mom knew that he had money and he said she did not. She just asked me if I could help her out with her rent because she was being evicted. I said, "Why did you give her all your money? Now you do not have money for the trip and your car. He looked at me with red teary eyes and said, "Miss Sandi, you can send me to respite until you all get back from Florida." I told him we were not going to do that, and we would loan him some money for the trip, but he was going to repay us, and he agreed. I could not get out of his room fast enough to telephone his mom, and when I did, I gave her a piece of my mind. She sounded like she was drunk. I am sure she was, always asking Richard for his money. There is something about all foster children, about 95% of the time they will always take up for their mothers. No matter what. We went to Florida, and they all had a blast. Memories that they could take with them.

Late August we were notified that Jaquan was aging out of the program and that he wanted to go back to New York where his family was. We wanted him to remain in Maryland and the agency was going to help him with his own apartment, but he insisted on returning to New York State. By the end of August Jaquan was gone, he would be missed by our entire family. Charlie would soon follow to a group home in Fort Washington, Maryland. He did not have active family, so Aaron and I were on his visitors list, and we saw him often and gave him money so he could buy extra from the vending machines. Just before Christmas, it was time for Richard to leave because he also aged out of the program. He went to live with his grandmother and soon moved in with a girlfriend. We would hear form Jaquan and Richard very often by telephone. Early one after noon Richard's mother phoned me and I could tell she was crying. She got as far as saying my name and I stopped her. I told her to call Aaron because I did not want to hear what she was going to say. I knew it was going to be bad. On Aaron's arrival home he told me that Richard's mom called him, I told him; "I knew that because she called me first and I told her to call you. "According to the information that Aaron received from Richard's mom, he was out drinking the night before with some of his friends. They apparently tried to take Richards keys form him so he could not drive himself home because he was drunk. He refused and started fighting with his friends. To make a long story short, Richard took his keys and went ahead out to his car to drive himself home. It was extremely late, and he knew he had to work in the morning. On the way home, he ran off the road into a big rock in front of someone's house and the car flipped over several times. He was not wearing a seat belt. His face was unrecognizable.

Aaron and I went to his funeral in Waldorf, Maryland, summer 2004. We were the only Black people at the service. We were a little bit apprehensive because Richard told us his dad was a Klansman a long time ago. We went to dinner with Jaquan and Richard and while we were waiting for our orders to be served Richard became teary eyed and I asked him what was wrong and he said, "I did not know that Black people do the same things that White people do. My dad told me a lot of awful stuff about Black people. "Richard's grandmother approached us at the service and asked if we were Richards foster parents and we told her that we were. She told us that Richard spoke often about us, and she appreciated that we were there for Richard when he needed someone. Richard's father also approached us. He hugged Aaron and thanked us for taking care of Richard. He said Richard loved our family. When we returned to our seats, Richard's Mom whom we were sitting with said, "I would never have believed my Ex would hug a Black man."

Jaquan called one day collect and I accepted the call. He told me that he was in prison and was given ten years for something he did not do. He went on to tell me that he was outside in the Bronx projects when a group of people got into an altercation and one-person was shot and killed. Everyone arrested when the police showed up. All were labeled as gang members. He said he was just out there like everyone else trying to see what was going on. He gave me information to his White female public defender who was trying to help him out and she wanted to speak with Aaron and me about what kind of person Jaquan was. We did that, she reopened his case, and had the conviction overturned. Jaquan moved out of the Bronx soon after his release. He met a White girl in New York City and they started a relationship. They were together for about two years and now had a child. He also had a child to a Black female in the Bronx projects where he was from. She heard about this other girl. She decided to have Jaquan murdered. I was notified by his White girlfriend who told me what had happened. Aaron and I drove to New York and attended Jaquan's funeral, October 2014. We were so sad. We met his mother and grandmother at the funeral service they thanked us for caring for him. We also told them that we would send pictures of Jaquan for their memories. His current girlfriend stayed in touch with us for about a year and we financially helped her out from time to time. We never heard from Charlie again.

CHAPTER FOURTEEN – Meet Rob, Lee, and Ricky

Rob and Lee both came about the same time. It was funny we lived in Roblee Acres. Rob was Latino and Lee was Black. Rob's funding agency was the Department of Juvenile Justice and Lee's was the Department of Social Services. Orienting them to the house went smoothly. Rob decided that he would call us Miss Sandi and Mr. Ace (Aaron's nickname) and Lee decided to call us mom and dad. They were both in the tenth grade and would attend Douglas High school. Rob was living with his dad and step mother, he had a counterfeiting and stealing habit. Lee had a mother who could not properly take care of her children. So, they were all removed. Settling in was no big deal, all went well? They got along with each other very well. Rob wanted to learn how to drive and we wanted him to learn, however, our program would not provide the money for driving school, nor would his dad. We were prohibited from allowing children to drive our automobiles because of insurance issues. We broke that rule on more than one occasion. Therefore, we went on to teach him to drive and we paid for his drivers classes. He drove very well. He passed the driving exam for his provisional license. That was great, for we were going on a trip to Disney in Florida for a summer vacation and he would be able to drive on the open road. We went on that trip at the end of the school year and we all had a great time. The boys enjoyed the vacation so much more than we did. We loved watching them having a great time. We went to several more parks before our planned trip back home.

Last day of the vacation came and it was time to pack and ride. Aaron drove the first few hours, then we decided that Rob would go next because we wanted him do his driving during the day light hours. He needed the experience. Rob was asleep in the back seat. So, I told

Aaron to pull over so we could get something to drink and go to bathroom. We took a quick break and it was time to go. I told Rob "You are up next." Oh my God, Rob started complaining and crying the Blues. "Miss Sandy I cannot drive I am too sleepy I cannot do it. If I drive, I know I might wreck and kill us all you do not want us all to die I am just sleepy I cannot drive I swear I cannot." I said, so little crying boy you want to drive so badly and suddenly you do not want to drive! To make a long story short he did not drive. Aaron and I completed the drive and were home before dark.

Summer was going well, and Rob was getting bored with school out and not much to do. I came home from work one evening and went to my office after settling down. I noticed a $100 dollar bill lying on my printer. I knew it did not belong to be. I yelled upstairs for Aaron to come to my office, and I showed him the $100 bill and he looked at it closely and knew it was counterfeit. Lee was in the recreation room across from my office and we asked him about it. He told us that Rob was making money for them. I was like, "Lord Jesus!" Lee said, "Mom I was not going to try to spend any of it." It was now time to approach Rob and when we did, he laughed and said he was just trying to see if he could make money and that he was not going to try to spend it. We decided that incident was something we would have to tell the case manager about this situation... We sat down had a long talk with Rob to explain to him that he could end up in jail with a felony charge. We did tell him that we were going to report that to the agency case manager it was that important to us. He pleaded for us not to tell and that he would not do it again, but I told him it was something we could not let go, we had to report it. Things seem to deteriorate with Rob and his behavior; we knew the honeymoon was over.

Rob always had something up his sleeve. One evening he came into my bedroom and sat down beside my small room safe. He looked over at me and said, "I bet I can open your safe." I just sat n looked at him. He started to turn the dial clockwise and looked at me and said, "Is the first number nine?" I continued to watch him, and he turned the dial the opposite direction and said, "Is the second number fifteen?" I got up, stopped him, and told him that if he kept up doing those sorts of things, he would end up in a real jail, not boy's village. He laughed and said, "I'm just playing Miss Sandi. He had the numbers correct.

We took a trip one weekend without the boys and my girlfriend Stephanie agreed to sit with the boys, she was a nurse that I worked with. Stephanie said that they gave her "a run for the money." On our arrival back home, Lee came into my bedroom later that evening and asked if everything was okay with our bedroom window. I asked what should be wrong with it. I walked around the corner to check our bathroom window and it was just sitting there. I called Lee and said to him, "what happened?" He said, "It wasn't my mom it was Rob." Oh Lord, I felt some kind of way about this boy. I called for Rob to come to my room. Lee made his way to the recreation room; he wanted no part of what was going to happen. When he presented, I asked him why our bedroom window was just sitting there without any locks in place, and he said to me "I just wanted to know if I could get in from the outside." I asked him if he found what he was looking for and he said, "I was not looking for anything." I told him that he was going to end up in place that was not going to be as nice as our house. I asked Aaron to have a long talk with Rob and he did. He later told me that he thought Rob was going to be one of the boys who would learn the hard way. He was nice and honest looking when we met him, but all children will take a honeymoon with you. Watching your every move and checking you out 24/7 until they know as much as they needed to know about you.

Rob would step up his unacceptable behavior. He would soon run away and convince Lee to go with him. We knew early on that Lee was the follower. He was a mama baby and Rob was street smart. The minute I realized that they were gone I phoned the Prince Georges County Police to report them as runaways. A police officer came to our house for a description of the boys and a picture of them as well. We always took a picture of all the children who came through our home. The boys were going for about three days when Lee decided he would call me. It was about 11:30 pm in the evening on a weekday. He called me collect from somewhere and I said where you are? He said, "I do not know where I am at mom, but Rob took us to one of his friend's houses and we were kicked out by the parents. So, I went into a store to ask If could use the phone to call you collect, I want to come home now." I told him to ask to use the phone and dial 911 so the police could come to pick him up; he said, "I do not know how to do that." I told him to dial 911 and tell them he was a runaway, and you need to get back home they will figure it out period. Not too long after I spoke with Lee, did the Montgomery County Police ring my phone and they wanted me to come and pick Lee up. I told them to call the P.G.C. Police for he was in their system. They did do that. Aaron and I received a call from the P.G.C. Police station in Upper Marlboro, Maryland where we picked Lee up about

2:00 in the morning. When he was escorted to our car, the police officer told him to be appreciative of the parents that he had. On the way home, Lee was noticeably quiet, and we did not ask him anything. On our arrival home, we told Lee to go to bed and to get some sleep for we would talk in the morning. We kept the on-call case manager up to date on the two runaways.

About six days in, Rob called me to talk, and I told him to turn himself it for things could only get worse. I told him that Aaron and I would come to pick him up, but he did not accept the offer. About ten days in and we received a call to let us know that our son Rob was incarcerated in Boys Village. We notified the agency and they handled it from there. Rob would spend two weeks in Boys Village and be released to us. When we went to pick him up, he came out to the desk where were to sign him out. When we got home, I asked Rob where he got the clothing that he was wearing, and he said' "when I went to the clothing closet to get my belongings, I left mine and took clothing that I liked." Aaron and I were too through with Rob. The next day we took the clothing back. We left Rob home and we returned the clothing that he had stolen from the clothing closet. When we returned home, he asked if we got his clothing for him. Well, the answer was hell no, you did not want your clothing, remember. I was about ready for school to start back up. They had too much free time.

Just before the opening day of school, the agency called us to accept a short-term placement. A young boy by the name of Rick, he was seventeen. He was Black and removed from his home because his mom tried to kill him by running over him with her automobile. We could hardly believe that a mom would do such a thing, but after living with Rick in our house for about two weeks, we could almost understand why. He was something else. Very respectful but never shut up. He said that he was going to go into the Air Force like his dad. I told him that he was going to have to learn to listen when someone was speaking to him. He got along fine with Rob and Lee. None of these three boys aged out. Rob went to a transitional group home with hopes of returning home to his dad. Lee went back home with his mom; she finally was approved to have her children back at home. Rick went back home for his dad was now back in country. He returned to his home school, finished a year later, and did go into the United States Air Force. Rob came to visit us about four years later. He now had a child and was in the United States Army. He said the judge in child support court gave him an option, military, or jail. He chose the army over jail. Lee would contact us about six years later; he was now a father with a child and was living with his girlfriend. We have not heard from any of them years past.

<u>CHAPTER FIFTEEN –Meet Chad and James</u>

The house has been quiet for a week or so and we needed the break. Then we would meet Chad, a White boy with blond hair and blue eyes, he was so sweet and quiet. The Department of Social Services was his funding agency. We knew that he would be honeymooning for a while. So, we would keep our guard up. He was out of school and his issues were with his father who was married to woman who was not his mom. He never told us anything about his parents or stepmother. Chad had a birthday coming up and he wanted to know if we could go out to dinner and if so, could his girlfriend come along. We saw nothing wrong with that for we would be present. We made plans and did go out on his birthday, his girlfriend's parents brought her over to our house, and we agreed to take her back home. While we were out to dinner, Chad's dad stopped by to pick him up for his birthday. He left a note and said that Chad knew he was going to pick him up for his birthday. I went into the kitchen where Chad was sitting with Aaron and I asked him if he had forgotten and he said, no, I did not want to be with him. We did not ask Chad to call and apologize to his dad for we knew that one of his issues was problems with dad.

Chad found a job working in Washington, DC, which means he had to take the metro to and from work. We provided his transportation to the metro. James would soon show up, he was nineteen and out of school, he was in placement awaiting transition to independent living in an apartment with a roommate. The Department of Social Services was his funding agency. He had a girlfriend with a baby and a car. Her baby belonged to his cousin. His visits with her were approved by the agency. He claimed he was looking for a job, but nothing ever panned out for him. He was with us long enough to go to Pittsburgh with Chad and us for Aaron's mom's birthday picnic. He was gone in less than forty-five days. That left Chad alone with us for the time being.

Almost every day when we drove Chad to the metro for work, he had his bag that he carried with him, hanging over his shoulder. I never thought to ask what was in the bag. Well, one day I was in the kitchen watching the news and there was a high-speed chase going on from P.G.C to

Waldorf, Maryland. They apprehended the man in the car.
I was so glad no one was injured. They said on the news, it
was a car stolen from the Addison Road metro. We
received a call from the police to tell us that the man in the
chase was our son, Chad. He was taken to P.G.C. Hospital
Emergency Room. When we got there, we were taken to
the cubicle where he was. He was handcuffed to the bed
and an officer was in the room. The officer told us that the
bag he had with him was now in custody for the active
crime. I asked the nurse who entered the area if he could
see a mental health physician, and they allowed it. Chad
was admitted to the mental health ward. A big part of being
a foster parent is being an advocate for the child, no matter
what. He was such an angry young man and he had so
many issues that he would not talk about. After being
released, from the hospital after a week or so and
transferred to a detention center, he would hang himself in
custody. We were so sad. In addition, it was a little
difficult to deal with. Luckily, there were no other foster
children in the home with us at the time and we were glad
about that. We received a call from the PGC Police
department to pick up his bag for they closed the case. We
were surprised when we looked inside the black bag.
Aaron said, "So, that is why I was missing so many of my
tools."

CHAPTER SIXTEEN –Meet Joey, Chris, and Leonard

Joey and Chris came about the same time. Joey was a
thin, tall young man who had a drug use problem and Chris
was a muscular young man with anger management issues.

Joey was a sweetheart. Both were White and got along okay together. The Department of Social Services was their funding agency. Joey was the quiet nice person who kept to himself and there were little issues with him. He would be temporary awaiting placement in a residential drug rehabilitation center. Yes, he had to go to drug counseling, like many of the foster children do. He would contact us about three or four years after he left and he informed us that he was living in York, Pennsylvania where I was born. He said he met a Black young woman in his drug rehab program and that they were in love and living together. He told me the young women's name and I told him that I did not know her, but I knew the family name. I wished him well and never heard from Joey again.

Chris on the other hand was a hand full. Things were going okay for a while, but he started to challenge Aaron and did not want to do anything he had to do. He had visitation rights with his grandparents who did not live to far from us and we transported him to see them on many occasions. One late evening, Chris butted heads with Aaron over some issue that I cannot recall nor is Aaron able to recall the incident. I heard the loud voices and went to see what was going on, but by that time Aaron had left the room, went outside, and got in his car. He returned soon with several boxes. He went into Chris' room, packed all his things, and told him he was leaving. Chris wanted to know where Aaron was going to take him, and Aaron told him to his grandparents' house. Chris was happy about that. It was after hours for our case manager, so we called the on-call case manager and told her what happened. Well, that was not the best move on our part. We were scolded and told that we were never to remove a child and take them to any person without permission and that if we wanted a child removed, we would have to give a thirty-day notice.

It would be about twenty years later when Chris reached out to me on social media. He messaged (November2021) me and said, "Miss Sandi do you remember me?" There was picture of him, his wife, and their child on his profile. I told him that I did not remember and to remind me of whom he was with. He did, and then I remembered. He said, "I was a hard one, right?" That was November 2021, just before thanksgiving. He is doing well. I guess he did hear some things that we said when he was living with us. We are now social media friends, as we are with many of our other foster children.

Joey and Chris were both now gone, and the house was quiet for a week or so, when we received a call to accept a nineteen-year-old Black male who was waiting for a spot in independent living. We did. His name was Leonard, and he was already working so we did not have to worry about that. We were not told of issues for Leonard, except that he was homeless. We had no issues moving forward, he went to work and kept his room neat. No drugs and no smoking issues.

CHAPTER SEVENTEEN – MEET MIKE

Mike was a seventeen-year-old Black male who was from Washington, DC and the goal was to keep him away from the gangs. The Department of Juvenile Justice was his funding agency. He was a short stocky young man and very mannerly. He was awaiting a spot for Job Corp. He would get along well with Leonard. They were both going to be short timers. During the time that they were there, I started a small home business and things were going okay. One day I made a sale. I was so excited about the sale that I framed the twenty-dollar bill. Aaron mounted the twenty-dollar bill in a frame and hung it on the wall. About a month in, I walked into my office and the twenty-dollar bill was missing. The frame was still there and hung up in its place, but the money was not. I was so hurt because I wanted to save it for good luck, you know. Mike swore he did not take it and so did Leonard. There was something about the way Leonard said that he did not do it. I just had a feeling that it was he. I was so ready for him to leave because he steals and that was not going to work for us. Soon both boys would be gone, and I was relieved that the agency transitioned Leonard to another program. Mike went to job Corp and Leonard to an independent living program.

We would never hear from Mike again, but Leonard showed up about five years later in a taxicab. I was surprised to see him when I opened the door. I invited him in, my grandson was visiting at the time, he was about ten, Keenan Jr. did not want to leave my side, but I told him it was okay because I knew Leonard. He did not go far. Leonard told me that the taxicab was his and that he was now living in Richmond Virginia with his girlfriend and their son. He stood up, took a twenty-dollar bill out of his wallet, and gave it to me. He confessed about taking the twenty-dollar bill and wanted to repay me. I told him that always felt that it was he and he said, "I know you did. I wanted to tell you for so long, so, today I decided to drive to Maryland and take a chance on seeing you and paying you back." I was so proud of him; he had become an honest man. That had to take a lot to do that. I could not wait for Aaron to come home to share that news. He was shocked too. We never saw Leonard ever again.

CHAPTER EIGHTEEN – Meet the Boy with Red Hair

For the life of me, I cannot remember this child's name nor can Aaron. It was the year 2003. He was a fifteen-year-old White male who was removed from his home because he threatened to kill his mother. The Department of Social Services was his funding agency. We went to meet him at the agency before accepting him. We wanted to see how big he was. If we could defend ourselves if we had to. He was a ridiculously small teenager with long blonde hair pulled back in a ponytail. I thought no big deal. Well, let me tell you, sometimes you must look at more than the size.

One evening I was home alone with this young man. It was about 9:30 p.m. and I knew his bedtime was 10:00 p.m. He was in the recreation room lying on the sofa watching television. I approached him and reminded him of his bedtime, and he told me that he knew what his bedtime was. It was now 10:05 p.m. and he was still lying on the sofa. I told him it was time for bed. He stood up and walked over to turn off the television and then he said I am going outside to smoke a cigarette first. I said nothing and walked away, back into my room. He came back into the house, came directly to my bedroom, and stood in the doorway. I was sitting on the floor next to my bed stuffing envelopes for my business. There was a step down when entering my room. He came in, sat down beside me, and started scolding me for not asking for help and I told him that I did not need any help. He started picking up envelopes, stuffing them, and telling me to ask for help the next time. Right under my bed was a machete that Aaron gave me just in case I ever needed it. I was hoping that he did not take me for his mom, he wanted to kill her. About 10:20 p.m. I heard Aaron's car pull into the driveway, boy was I happy about that. He came in, walked to our room, looked at the boy, and said it is time for your bedtime. He stood up quickly and said, "Mr. Ace I was on my way to bed." That night I told Aaron that I was a little concerned about him and that I was not sure this placement would work out for me.

The next day while I was at work, Aaron phoned me to tell me that our foster son dyed his hair red. He told me that he had gotten red hair dye all over the bathroom and that he had him clean it all up. When I arrived home and saw him, all I thought about was how he looked just like Chares Manson. We put our thirty-day notice in and never ever heard from him again. That was okay.

CHAPTER NINETEEN – Meet Kinney

Kinney, a Black eighteen-year-old male about six feet tall, funded through the Department of Social Services. He was being groomed for the independent living program in our agency, Alternatives for Youths and Families. Orientation and expectations were the first order of business. It was summer when he arrived, and our grandson Keenan was with us for a few weeks during that time. He came for visits often. Kinney was to find employment and with our help, he did about two miles from our house. He would always walk because he did not want to spend his allowance or money that he earned. He would be the first foster child that we would give a prepaid spending card for we had given our grandson one and did not want him to feel any kind of way. They did not share rooms and it was a good thing. It would be soon that I realized that Kinney was a bed wetter. By the time, I figured it out that he was a bed wetter the mattress was ruined. We had to buy another one and with our own funds. I knew that Kinney and I would have to come up with a plan to break this behavior.

 I discussed the issue with Aaron and then I sat down with Kinney and discussed with him my plan to help him, and he agreed to it. 1) There was to be no fluids taken in after six o'clock p.m. 2) I would wake him up four hours after he went to bed and then four hours after he went back to bed. He also had to get up early and clean the linen if he had an accident during the night. By the time, he left our home to move on to independent living in a shared apartment with another independent living foster child, he would no longer be a bed wetter. Kinney, Aaron, and I kept that to ourselves. His Department of Social Services case manager had already known about it but never shared it with our agency. Kinney and I would have many conversations during his time with us. He shared that his mother was addicted to drugs for as long as he could remember. She would take him to the grocery store to steal meats to sell for drugs. He told me that she would stuff the meat inside of his jacket in the food cart and that it made him so cold and that was why he rolled up in his blankets at night, putting them between his legs, so that when he wet, he did not feel cold, it made him feel warm. I thought that was so sad, poor child.

Work for Kinney was going well. He was saving his money as planned. One day our grandson told me his debit card was missing. After looking for it all over Keenan's room, I decided to ask Kinney if he had it because Keenan said he took it. I asked Kinney and he confessed. He had no reason as to why he did it. However, he gave it back to Keenan and l told him he would have to repay the money that he spent from the card, and he did. That was the first and last time for stealing. It would be about six months later and time for Kinney to leave. He transitioned out to independent living in another Maryland county. Aaron would run into him about ten years later. He told Aaron that he was doing well, working and in love with a schoolteacher in Calvert County, Maryland. That was the last contact.

CHAPTER TWENTY – Meet Verge and Tim

Verge was Black and removed from his adoptive parents' home. He had a twin sister as well who was doing well at home. Tim on the other hand was tall and thin. He was White and was removed from his mom's house for unruly behavior. The Department of Social Services was their funding agency. It was now 2004 and we had sold our home and moved to another part of Maryland. Both in high school and would be attending Crossland High. We did not know that either of the boys had a history of stealing, but we would find out very soon. They both called us Mr. Ace and Miss Sandi. About six months in, we started getting complaints from school about Verge. He was always getting into something, skipping classes, etc. One afternoon we received a call from the Giant food store, which was across the street from the high school. Aaron and I both went to the store to speak to the security officer who phoned us. On our arrival, we were told that Verge had been coming to the store and stealing on a routine basis. They showed us pictures of him on the security cameras running out of the store. The officer also told us that he chased Verge but could not catch him. The younger officer who was present said, "he got away from the old guy, but let him try that on me, I will catch him." We were told that his picture would be hung up in the store and that he was never to come into the store ever again.

We were wondering how we were going to move forward with this young man. The children in the system seem to be much harder to deal with. We notified the case managers in our program and his funding agency. We all agreed to some rules for Verge, and he signed and agreed to them. That was short lived. Aaron would notice that in the garage where he had a five-gallon water jug filled up with change that he had been saving for several years was gone. The whole jug was empty. He was furious. We called both boys to a meeting with us, when they came home from school and asked them both about the missing money. Tim looked at us and said, "Miss Sandi and Mr. Ace I do steal, but I would never still from you because we are family now. I have that much respect" He looked at Verge and said, "Man you need to confess." Verge just sat there and did not say anything. That was enough for us to decide that we did all we could do for Verge. He transitioned from our house within a few weeks.

Things were going well with Tim. I respected his feelings about family. He passed to 12th grade and had not been into any trouble that we were aware of at the time. He was being released to his father, stepmother, and siblings. He was transferred to his home of record in Calvert County, Maryland. We were invited to his graduation. In 2013, we would hear from Tim again. He was now incarcerated on a drug charge. We keep in tough and send him money for things that he needs twice a year. We still believe that he can become a law abiding, contributing citizen if give the opportunity when he completes his term of incarceration. He always wanted to be an artist and he could always draw very well. It was a dream of his. We believe that if he can visualize it, he will achieve it one day.

CHAPTER TWENTY-ONE– Meet Jerome

Jerome was an eighteen-year-old Black male, tall and handsome. He was from Baltimore, Maryland. The Department of Juvenile Justice was his funding agency. It did not take much time for him to find a job. He did very well with us, but wanted to move back to Baltimore against everyone's better judgement. Because he was once affiliated with a gang in Baltimore. He was with us for about a year and did go back to Baltimore. We would hear from him about a year after he left. He had his own apartment and was working in an apartment complex in janitorial services. We never heard from him again.

CHAPTER TWENTY-TWO – Meet the Boy Who Would Not Shower

Miss Patti Duncan a foster parent in our agency had a young boy who would not shower, no matter what. She asked the agency and us if we could take him temporarily, at least until he took a shower because his body odor was horrible. I do not know anything about him except he was a White teenage boy who would not shower. He would be with us a couple of weeks. I do not know how Aaron convinced him to shower but he did. He took quite a few showers in that brief period. Patti was happy and we were glad to help. In the agency, Alternatives for Youths and Families, it was a fact that Patti Duncan and the Stockton's took the complicated cases.

CHAPTER TWENTY-THREE – Meet Kaphono and Timothy

It was now 2009. Kaphono was Black and Timothy M. was white. Tim told us his nickname was Jason Borne and that Dog the bounty hunter was his cousin so no one would beat him up. Both funded by Department of Social Services. Timothy was in the twelfth grade and Kaphono had a diploma that never looked quite real. We would later find out that it was not genuine. Kaphono was coming from his single parent home with his mom, and Timothy was coming from another foster parent's home that was in our agency. He told his foster parent, Patti that he wanted to live with the Stockton's. Patti called us and told us that Timothy told her that he wanted to live with Mr. Ace. We told her it would be fine if the agency agreed and they did.

Kaphono was to find work to ready himself for independent living in an apartment of his own. That was interesting. I registered Timothy for school at Doctor Henry A. Wise Jr. High school with no issues. He would be taking the school bus. We were in the process of building a new home in Upper Marlboro, Maryland and knew having two boys was going to take some planning.

Kaphono found a job at one of the fast-food restaurants as a busser and all he did was complain. The first week he complained that the servers were not helping him to clean the tables. He said, "all they do is bring their food to them and I have to do the dirty work." We tried to explain what busser meant. It obviously did not work because he quit the job soon after he started. It was not even thirty days. Now we were back to job-hunting again. Job number two, working at a mattress warehouse. Lord, he complained so much, telling us that he had to lift mattresses by himself and no one was helping him. Aaron asked him if the other people had help and he said no, but they have been there for a long time, I am still learning. Now he had a bright ideal that he wanted to be a male stripper. When Aaron told him he would have to take off his clothes, he decided that he did not want to do that. Then a bouncer at a club etc. Aaron told him he would have to fight sometimes when people did not want to leave the club. He decided that he did not want to do that either.

Three months in and we had all we could take from this young man. His mother contacted the agency to tell them that Kaphono had an uncle in New Jersey and he was willing to have him come to live with him in New Jersey but he would have to work. Kaphono wanted to go there to see his uncle. The agency contacted his uncle and arranged a time for the visit and we drove him to see his people. There were three row houses on and old country road. We found the uncle and he told us the other houses were all relatives of Kaphono. Kaphono ask to go to the bathroom and it was an outhouse. He was not happy about that. On the way back to Maryland, he decided that he did not want to move with his uncle. So, he was transitioned out of our house to a group home. We would hear from him about three years later and he wanted to know if he could use our address for his mail and I told him no. He never called us again. We were too busy to deal with any shenanigans from him. Timothy went to the property and helped us many times working on the road to the new house.

Timothy had grandparents who lived a few minutes from us. We contacted them and to arrange for him to visit them on a routine basis while he was with us. Timothy had a mother in the area that was married but her husband did not want him. Timothy was getting good grades in school. He had good book sense. He learned somewhere that the man of the house is in charge and anything that I wanted him to do he had to clear with Aaron. One day I asked him to do something, I cannot remember what it was, but he looked at me and asked me if I checked with Mr. Ace. I looked at him with a serious look and I said, "I am going to ask you one more time!" That was all it took; I had no more issues. He found out that a woman could also be in charge as well. The rest of the year went rather quickly and Timothy graduated high school. He told us he was going to work on being a storm chaser. I do not think he ever did that. It was soon time for him to leave for he finished high school. We have been in contact with Timothy ever since he left our home. He is married with three children and one on the way. When he left in June of 2009, we decided to not take any more children for a while. We were concentrating on completing our new home.

CHAPTER TWENTY-FOUR – Meet Luis, Jonathan, and Kyle

It is now November 2009 and we just moved into our brand-new home built from the ground up on twenty-seven acres, our dream home. We had planned to not accept any more children for a while. We had settlement in our new home along with the loan officer. We had no furniture, but we decided to sleep on the floor with blankets in our new house. It was big and spooky with no curtains and all kinds of strange noises on the farm. The next morning, we sat on the front porch just talking about the journey it took to get where we were. Well to make a long story short we received a call about thirty days after moving into the new house. The agency had a fourteen-year-old Latino boy that they needed to move from his father's house. His name was Luis and the goal was to get him to his mother in Florida. He was an immigrant and came to this country with his aunt who promised his mother she would get him across the border. She did, but she took him to his dad's house. His dad was illegal himself and was married. The wife did not like Luis and kept at him, causing his dad to beat him often over something she would tell him about Luis. The school reported the father and Luis was removed from his home and placed into the foster care system. Luis was in ninth grade when he came to live with us. He would stay for about a year and then moved to Florida with his family. He was so sweet, and we have been in contact since he left. We did visit him in Florida on more than one occasion. We met his mom, siblings, and step farther. Stepfather was a legal resident, but mom was not. We are in touch by social media as well. He would see us off and on for he did come to Maryland to visit his father and he would bring him to visit us.

While he was with us, we accepted another boy who was seventeen and White. He would go to the same school that Luis was attending, Gwen Park High School. Both boys funded by the Department of Social Services. Jonathan and his siblings were removed from his home with a single parent who could not care for them adequately. The father was deceased. Luis was doing well in school, but Jonathan was not doing anything but holding a seat. I bought a PS2 for Luis to use while at our home and I told him to never take it to school. Well, that went over his head. One day he allowed Jonathan to hold it. Jonathan took it to school and told Luis it was stolen. We never believed that, we felt that Jonathan sold it. We never found out the true story. We never bought another one, we learn fast. When the school year ended, Luis went to Florida for the permanent move. Jonathan would remain and we would start talking to the agency about a different plan for Jonathan for he was not interested in school. Whatsoever.

Once Luis left, we accepted another boy, Kyle. Seventeen-year-old White boy who would be going to Gwen Park with Jonathan. He was funded by the Department of Juvenile Justice Services. We gave both boys a prepaid spending card for it would be easier for their use in school. One-day Jonathan's card came up missing and Kyle took it. That was easy to find out because I could see purchases online from the store next to their school. We had experience with this sort of thing in the past. Kyle did pay him back. Kyle was doing well in school, but Johnathan kept telling me he was not feeling it. Therefore, Aaron and I requested a team meeting to decide what to do about Jonathan's schooling. The team decided that we would register Jonathan for GED schooling. So, we did. Things started to move along simply fine.

We met Jonathan's family, mother, grandmother, and his uncle Billy. We also met his siblings that were in another foster home, but all were together. We had Jonathan buy Christmas gifts for his siblings while he lived with us. We also met Kyle's parents, they were kind, and his mom was in the army. He had two little sisters that we also met. It would not be long before Jonathan was leaving us. His uncle Billy requested to have Jonathan move with him and his wife and he did, all went well. Kyle was transitioned back to his family. Kyle is in a relationship and has three children. Jonathan is married and has four children we are in contact constantly with Jonathan and Kyle.

CHAPTER TWENTY-FIVE – Meet Sam

A seventeen-year-old Black male funded by The Department of Social Services. He was such a lovable character. Their adopted father was overwhelmed as a single father. Therefore, he asked to have them all placed temporary from his home. Sam's mother when she was extremely ill and in a nursing, home asked a nurse if she would adopt her boys before she died. The nurse convinced her husband that they should adopt the boys, four of them. One set of twins. They did. The adopted mother died while the biological mother was still alive. After the death of the adopted mother, things went so wrong. The boys were getting into a lot of trouble in school and other places and dad could not take it.

He was a retired military man and kept insurance on all the boys, so they had good medical care available to them. We had many conversations with dad about the boys. One of the twins was doing terrible things. But at least Sam was away from all of them. Sam was in high school at Gwynn Park. I used to play old music and Sam knew all the words and I asked him where he learned them from, and he told me his adoptive mom used to play old records and he learned. He told me she also taught him and his brothers how to dance. I tried him out and yes, he could dance rather well. He did well with us. He aged out into a shared apartment with another foster boy. We thought that was a mistake for he was not ready and did not graduate yet. Aaron and I went to Charles County to visit him one day and the apartment was a mess. We stayed there for a while, helped him to clean it up, and told him and his roommate if they continued to live like that; they would get rodents and forced to move from the apartment. We would hear from Sam about one year later for his high school graduation. We were happy that he made it. So, we went to his graduation, and he was speaking, and he thanked us for being his foster parents for he said he might have not ever graduated from high school if it were not for us. We were very happy. We are in touch with Sam on social media, especially when he needs something.

CHAPTER TWENTY-SIX - Meet William, Lek, Charles, and the Thirteen-Year-Old Runaway

It is now 2013 and children keep coming. William a thirteen-year-old White male and Leke a seventeen-year-old Black male. William arrived first and there were no issues until Leke arrived. They were both in school attending Gwen Park High School. They were in separate bedrooms in our house. They were both funded by the Department of Social Services. One from Baltimore County and one from Calvert County, Maryland. William and his three siblings were being cared for by their mother. They were homeless. All the children were split up. Our daughter ended up getting Williams's younger brother, so they lived next door to each other and saw each other almost daily. The goal was for William and his siblings to be placed with family. His younger sister was with an aunt and his older brother was in a group home. The agency and the foster care team set up monthly visits for the children and their mother was invited. The fathers of the children were absent. We, the foster parents, and caregivers for the children all met in Bowie, Maryland at a park monthly.

That kept the children in touch with each other. Thomas
would be with us for about two years. His brother was
moved from our daughter's house next door because the
agency wanted to put him in a mental health facility for
treatment. Our daughter, Karmentrina went to Baltimore to
visit him weekly for no one else was, not even the social
workers. When it was finally time to release him, he could
not go back to Karmentrina's house because she had
accepted a foster female. So, she convinced me to take him
until she could get him back or he went to his paternal
grandmother's home who was trying to get custody for a
long time.

Leke had a grandmother in Orlando, Florida and his
agency set up visits for him with the grandmother.
Grandmother was Jehovah Witness and decided she could
not handle Leke. So, then the plan changed to job corp.
Leke was interested. He was with us for about a year until
a slot opened for him. During that year, we put him in a
driver's training classes and he left us with his driver's
license. We were incredibly happy about that. I caught
him sharing cigarettes with William and I let him know that
I was unhappy about that. He started talking back about
this and that. It was certainly time for him to leave us. We
went to see him on visitation days and on holidays. About
a year, after Leke was there he called me to tell me that he
was no longer in Job Corp because a female accused him of
inappropriate behavior, and we were not surprised. That
was the last we heard from Leke and we were okay with
that.

One day before Leke left, I was sitting in my room and decided that I would have a glass of wine. To my surprise, it was water. Then I checked several other bottles and the bottles were all filled with water. I approached William and Leke and asked them who entered my room and drank all my wine. Of course, no one had an answer. We had a combination battery operated lock on our door. They refused to tell me how they were getting into our room. Therefore, I called the Prince Georges County Police Department and told them my situation. They sent two officers to my house. After a little bit of persuasion, William told them how they entered my bedroom door. After that, we put in a floor lock and that took care of that problem. Now we lost all trust in William. We counted all the bottles and charged them both at five dollars a bottle. A lot less than it all cost. So, we took a trip to the ATM and withdrew the money they owed us from their prepaid spending cards. We asked William to be removed and within thirty days, he was moved to another foster parent. We continued to see him monthly at the agency monthly meetings. Leke left for the job corps a few days before William left. Both were gone and just in time for Charles to come home with us. Charles was living with us but was over at Karmentrinas more than he was home with us. He could not spend the nights there because she had foster girls. He would not be with us exceptionally long because his grandmother was finally granted physical custody of him and William. She now had both boys and was still trying to get the older brother.

Allow me to introduce you to the thirteen-year-old runaway. He was a Black male. If we had known that he had a history of being a runaway, we would not have accepted him. He also had tantrums. He would just stand there looking at you and shaking his head. He would not speak. He would be with us for a noticeably short time. One afternoon my great niece Caprecia was on her way home from my house, when she saw our foster son crossing the railroad track about a half mile from our house. She called me and said he was wearing his headphones and walking and rocking his head. I got in my car and drove to the area where she saw him and tried to get him to get into the car and he would not. I went back home and called his case manager who drove from Baltimore to get him. By the time she arrived, he had walked back to our house and was sitting in the yard. Miss Patricia, our agency case manager tried to get him to get into her car for about two hours. It was getting dark and I told her to leave because he knew his way to his bedroom. She left. About thirty minutes after she left, he found his way to his bedroom, got in bed, and went to sleep. The next morning the case manager phoned me and said that the agency was going to remove him from our home and put him in a residential treatment facility. The next day, they came for him. Miss Patricia and a male agency worker came to pick him up.

About a week or so after he was removed from our home, I noticed that my Bose charger was missing. I phoned the agency and told them about it. They said they would check to see if he had it. They said they asked him and he denied taking it, but later when they did a room search, it was found. I was incredibly happy about that. About a month later, the agency told Aaron and me that the boy was no longer in the residential treatment facility because he kept running away from there. Next, he was admitted to a locked facility. I was told the back-story on this boy months later. He and his siblings locked in a basement for months and he was the oldest of the children. He would crawl out of the window at night to look for food for himself and his siblings. I often

think about him and wonder what happened to him and his
siblings.

CHAPTER TWENTY-SEVEN - Meet Little Brother and Big Brother

It is now 2016 the agency asked us if we would take two
brothers. Ages seven and ten years old. Third grade and
sixth grade. They were White and funded by the
Department of Social Services in Saint Mary's County. We
had to think about that for a while. The brothers placed in a
family in our organization before coming to us. We would
first meet them early September when they were removed
from their foster home for an investigation. The little
brother said his foster mom hit him. He had identifiable
marks on his arm that the first-grade schoolteacher noticed,
and she reported it. The accusation was unfounded, and the
boys went back to their foster home. About six months
later, another accusation came up and the boys came to us
again. This time it was permanent.

This was unfamiliar territory for us because we always took
teens. Now we would have to walk them to the bus stop,
which was at the end of our quarter of a mile driveway.
Aaron and I took turns. They would be with us for about
two years. We took it upon ourselves to ask the previous
foster mother if she had any pictures of the children
because she had them for some time. The boys told me
before I called her that there would be no pictures of them.
So, I called her. She told me that there were no pictures of
the boys, not even on holidays and they had been with her
for a couple of years. We decided at that point that we

would build a life book for both boys, so that when they left us, they would have many memories to remember.

We were in and out of court with their mom trying to get custody of them. In the meantime, we met little brothers' biological paternal grandparents who had been trying to get custody of their grandson for years, but the agency kept denying them because big brother had no family, and they did not want to separate them. I told the grandparents that Aaron and I would help them to fight for their grandson. We did and they eventually received full custody of him. I spoke up for them in court and explained to the judge that we would be willing to have little brother at our home at least once a month and a week or so in the summers as long as big brother was with us. He agreed and it was done.

It was about five month or so when we started to have problems out of big brother. He was lonely because we had no children in our house. We registered him at the prince Georges recreation center and took him there for basketball camps, etc. That did not help very much. Big brother did not make friends easily, even at school. He had never invited anyone over to our house. I finally had a conversation with his case manager from our agency and his funding agency that I thought he needed to be in a home with other children. We had a new foster family who had recently come on board, and they had a son about two years younger than big bother. The agency setup a meet time and big brother wanted to go. He went with them and is still there today. We saw him often at first and then every now and then, because our daughter Kimmy is a respite foster parent and when he is with her, we go over to her house to visit him. He is all grown up now, twelfth grade and has a car that Department of Social Services bought for him.

Little brother and grandparents are doing well. I made contact with them this month to wish them a happy holiday and a happy New Year in 2022.

CHAPTER TWENTY-EIGHT – One Must Know When to Quit

Court appointments, therapy sessions, medical appointments, case manager appointments, agency meetings, Department of Justice meetings, Department of Social Services meetings, school, teacher parenting meetings, sleepless nights and so very much more. Aaron and I decided that we were done after little brother and big brother. We did not want to quit completely so we decided to give our notice and switch to respite care only for the time being. We were burned out from the independent living and high school age children. For almost half of our marriage, we have had children to care for, our own, nieces, nephews, cousins, and friends to look out for in our lifetime. That with over one hundred foster children is enough. Now we are jumping into our car whenever we want to without letting anyone know or requesting care for our foster children. We were really enjoying life for about three months, and then came a call.

CHAPTER TWENTY-NINE - Meet Five-Year-Old Johnny

The call was for respite for a five-year-old for two days. I was now 70 years old and to think of anyone who was not even in school was a bit much. Our daughter Karmentrina was spending the weekend with us, so I decided that she could help us if we needed her to. From the moment, that little cute White boy entered the house it was on. I do not know what he was running on, but his energy level was over the top. The case manager told me not to believe all the stories that he would share with us because he was good at it. For starters, he told us his mom was dead and his dad was trying to get him out of foster care. We would find out later from the foster parents that his mom was not dead and his dad incarcerated. He never stopped running around the house, at one point he followed me upstairs to my bedroom where he ran in and did a summersault over my bed. I just knew he was going to hit his head on the television stand, but he missed it. He was only at our house for a few hours, and we had two whole days to go. His foster parents were to meet us in Bowie on Sunday morning. That could not come quick enough. It was getting near dinnertime and I asked him what kind of food he wanted, and he wanted pizza. That was great, we had pizza. I told him that he had to get a bath before bedtime, and he wanted to know if he could bathe himself because the foster parents always did it and he was big enough to take a bath by himself. I told him I would think about it. Later after dinner, I heard him ask Karmentrina if he could take a bath in the room where she was because he did not want Miss Meany to do it. He was referring to me. Laugh aloud. He was referring to me. I was so incredibly happy that she said she would take care of it. He told her he wanted bubbles in the tub. It seemed like he would never get sleepy for bed after that bath. I sat him up for bed about nine p.m. in a guest room with a television and he would not get sleepy he wanted to know if he could sleep in the guest room with Karmentrina. We agreed and when he fell asleep, Aaron moved him to the upstairs guest room for the night. One night down and one more to go. I left the television on in his room. I know that when I fall asleep with the television and someone decides to turn it off, I wake up. Karmentrina fell in love with the little guy. She told the agency that she would do respite care for him after she completed her bachelor's degree, which graduation was coming soon. We would find out later from the agency case manager that the little boy was institutionalized. So, sad!

CHAPTER THIRTY – 2019 Retirement for the Stockton's

At the annual Board of Child Care, (They took over for Alternatives for Youths and Families) event, we told the agency that we were retiring from that day on, and we did. December 2019 and done. I knew Aaron was more tired of taking care of children than I was because he also worked in the children's group homes when they were short of staff. I put my energy into writing books, and this is one of them. We have shared our most memorable foster care stories with you. Although we have had many more children than we spoke of, we are not at liberty to discuss their stories. We hope that our stories will encourage you to consider caring for a foster child in your home. So many children need to be cared for. There is always something more than hope that a foster parent can give. Do not think too long, there is a child waiting to meet you. **_Remember_**, there is always room for one more.

REFLECTIONS

Donna Bowers-Bennett!

I came to work at Alternatives for Youth and Families in December 1993 after graduating that May with a Master's in Social Work. One of the first foster families I met was Ace and Sandy Stockton. I was a therapist in the Crisis Program. Children in that program were either being discharged from an adolescent psychiatric unit or a residential treatment center and were awaiting their next placement or were moving to a higher level of care such as a Residential Treatment Program and needed a place to be until they were admitted. These children required placement immediately, generally within hours. There was no extended review of paperwork or interviewing process. We got the call found an available foster parent and moved the child in. Not all foster parents could or would take children this quickly, sight unseen and sometimes in the middle of the night. The Stockton's did. These were children with challenging behaviors and mental health issues, often from complex family systems. The one thing that I noticed with every child that the Stockton's took in was a philosophy that goes something like this. You have crossed the threshold of my home; you are now family.

One of the tenets that I have always felt was especially important as a social worker or as a foster parent is to recognize that regardless of the family these children came from and the issues that they may have had, most of these children loved their family and wanted to return to them someday. To work with these children, you must respect their feelings for their family of origin. That respect is often the way to reach that child. I found that the Stockton's were able to do that effectively. They would take children in and treat them like their own while never losing sight of the family that child came from. They went the extra mile to include family members of the children, to mentor them and help them grow so that they could maintain the relationship with their child, even if the child did not return to them. You have crossed the threshold; you are now family.

Over the years our programs expanded, and I moved to various positions in the agency, spending the bulk of my time there as the Clinical Director. The Stockton's took in children for short term placements of 30 days or less and long-term placements: some a year or more. Some of the children would move on to other placements, return home, or have to go to different programs to provide treatment for their mental health issues. Some would come and go several times from our programs and from the Stockton's home. When a child returned to our agency that had been in their home before, they were there to welcome them and support them. You have crossed the threshold; you are now family.

In my role as Clinical Director, I would often interview children for placement in our different programs. These kids often knew each other and would talk about their experiences in different placements. Frequently, during an interview, I would talk to the child about the family that we were looking to place them in. When I would mention the

Stockton's often, they would know, by word of mouth, who they were. "I've heard they are really nice, and it would be a great place to go, my friend told me about them." This was often echoed by their caseworker from the Department of Social Services or Department of Juvenile Services who would accompany them to interviews, along with a sigh of relief as they saw their job being just a bit easier with that placement. You know people from the family; you are now family too.

Our agency operated two therapeutic group homes, one for boys, and one for girls. Some of these children did not have a family they could visit with, spend Christmas with, or interact with as they moved through the program. The Stockton's would often take these children in for a weekend respite, to hang out with a family for a while and have a break. As time went on and Ace retired from the Air Force Active Duty he had a little more time on his hands, he would pick-up shifts at the group homes and would do maintenance work when needed. He would include the residents in what he was doing; teaching new skills and talking with them; modeling for them appropriate adult and youth interactions. Many of these children did not have male role models or father figures in their lives and Ace provided them one to interact with and learn. I have crossed the threshold of your home and you are family.

As our programs continued to grow and we brought on more foster parents, it became evident that the new foster parents needed people to mentor them in their role. As a social worker, I could talk about mental health, family interaction, behavior management etc..... Sometimes what they really needed was someone who had been there to talk to about the day-to-day realities of being a foster parent. There were a couple of families we picked to be mentors in the program. The Stockton's were at the top of that list. Even though they had been fostering parents for years at that point, they always came to trainings offering their knowledge and more importantly their support to new parents. "Hey, just call us if you got a question." They would offer their home for respite for children whose foster parents needed a break so that the child would not be permanently disrupted from their placement. Foster children have crossed the threshold of your home; we are now family too.

The Stockton's had no criteria for the children placed in their home. It did not matter their race, their religion, their family of origin or male or female. They took them in. There was no judgement about who these children were. They were just children in need. Over the years, these children would come and go. But there was never a time when I saw or Ace or Sandy that I did not hear, "Donna, remember (enter name here)? They called the other day, and this is what they are doing." There were lots of stories of success and some troubling times, but they were always excited to hear from them. These kids would call on Mother's Day, Father's Day, Christmas or just because. They would bring their own children to meet the Stockton's. Often, when times get rough, these kids would reach out for a kind word, some guidance, and support. The Stockton's were there. You may have crossed back over my threshold, but you are still family.

Even when tragedy would strike their own family, the Stockton's kept their foster kids with them. Always recognizing that these children are watching every move and being included is of paramount importance. Not only did it impact Ace and Sandy and their children it impacted the wider family. Always modeling always teaching. It was here you saw the true value of their work, as children from the past showed up for them when they needed it. We are a family, and we will get through this together.

I worked at Alternatives for Youth and Families for 17 years. I left as the Executive Director. When I moved on to my own private practice, the Stockton's were still there, taking in children and supporting families. Over the years, our paths have crossed thanks to social media. They are still out there supporting the children many are well into adulthood. Sometimes, I see them post a message of support or gentle guidance, and I smile. The true impact of what the Stockton's have done for children can never be truly measured. I do know that the ripples are far reaching and will impact generations. I have worked with children and families as a Social Worker for nearly 30 years. If there is a lesson that we could all learn from the Stockton's example it is this: Accept the people that cross your threshold, do not judge them but respect their differences, give them the best you have in good times and in bad. What a wonderful human family we would be if we could all do that.

Donna Bowers Bennett LCSW-C

Coaching for the Voyage

<u>Memories from Michelle!</u>

I was 13 years old when I moved in with Mama Sandi and Poppa Ace. I remember walking into their beautiful home and instantly feeling like I was home. I have so many fine memories of my time with them. I loved how they would decorate for Christmas, as Christmas is my favorite time of the year. The living room upstairs was as a winter Wonderland and the whole table filled with Christmas village ornaments. It was simply gorgeous. I remember thinking that one day I wanted to have a village like that in my home for my family.

I remember Kimmy Jo and Karmentrina helping me to get ready for homecoming and helping me tame my hair because the kids at school would make fun of my hair. I remember them talking to me and telling me to not let others influence how I feel about myself. There are so many life lessons that I have carried with me into my adulthood. I also, remember a time when we had gone to a wedding convention as Karmentrina was getting married. I had called Mama Sandi mom, and a passing White woman said to mom; "how is she your daughter she's white?" Mama Sandi told her that I was her daughter and to mind her own business (if I remember correctly). I remember feeling so very proud at mama Sandi calling me her daughter.

When I was turning 14 when Poppa Ace surprised me with tickets to Garth Brooks, I knew he was not a fan, but I was touched that he would be willing to take me. I was so excited to go, and I loved it. Poppa took a nap during the concert, but it is something that I will always remember.

This occasion like many others showed me that night that I was important to people that I mattered. I was loved!!! As a foster child, you do not always get that, but I got that from them, and I truly believe it has changed the course of my life. I value the morals that they instilled in me, and I love that they showed me. I could not have asked for better foster parents. I know I was not always the easiest of children to raise. The second time that I stayed with them my foster sister Jennifer and I snuck out of the house. I remember us talking about sneaking out and I was so scared to go. I knew that it was wrong, and I was scared to hurt Mama and Poppa. I wish I could say that I didn't go but I did. I don't remember how long we were gone but I remember feeling so ashamed. It was a lesson to me to not let others persuade me to do something I really did not want to do. Even after that, they still showed me love and compassion.

Mama Sandi and Poppa Ace picked me up when I was feeling down, taught me many of life's lessons when they needed to be taught. They helped me to build a foundation when I had nothing to stand on. They helped me to become the woman I am today and gave me everything I needed to build a life of my own and for that, I would always be grateful to the Stockton's. Love Michelle!

Michelle W., First Foster Daughter

A Note from Kimmy Jo Kearse!

I am the daughter of Sandra and Aaron Stockton. I always knew I wanted to be a social worker of some sort and adopt kids, but foster care was never on my mind. When my parents started doing foster care, I became involved by helping them with their foster children. Mom suggested that my baby sister Karmentrina and I consider getting involved since we were so involved with helping them. I thought about it and decided that I would try.

I called the agency, Alternatives for Youths and Family, and made an appointment to speak with someone there. I was familiar with some of their case managers already. I agreed to go through the orientation, and it went well. I was familiar with the rules of helping my parents. A few weeks after my orientation, I was invited to be a foster parent to my first foster child, a boy. He was older than my son was and that placement did not work out very well.

Therefore, I decided to be a foster parent to girls only. I did not want my son being jealous and butting heads with boys for my attention. Finally, I was convinced to meet a little girl who was in a group home in Baltimore. Her name is Dejuanna. I fell in love at first sight. She was sweet as can be and I decided to take a chance. After about four months, the honeymoon is over. That is the period when the child is on their best behavior.

I was new to this, and it was overwhelming, but I had a family to help and lots of therapy and therapist for her. She was 11 when I met her, and she had a sister in the system as well, Jada whom I would request to get her in my home for visits, so they could see each other often. A few years later Jada came to live with me I ended up adopting both. They are now a permanent part of my family. They are now ages 24 and 19.

I met them both at 11 and 8. They found their forever family with us. Foster care is not an easy job, but it is rewarding because you touch the lives of many in positive ways that help them to survive in this world. I have fostered many school-age girls through the years. Quite a few are still in my life today.
I am still actively doing foster care. It is sad because we need so many more people to step up. This is not the easiest job to do, but someone must do it. We must try to save this generation of lost children.

Kimmy J. Kearse – Daughter of the Author
Adoptive foster parent

<u>**Reflections from Karmentrina Kearse!**</u>

I remember when my parents first decided to become Foster Parents. My mom had seen a news report about fostering a girl who was pregnant that needed immediate care. She had submitted their names and her eyes filled with excitement as she shared the story with me. Once contacted by the agency, another family had taken that child. Nonetheless, they had other children that needed placement. Therefore, my parents decided to try it. Since my siblings and I were all grown up and moved out of the house, I wondered if they were experiencing "Empty Nest Syndrome." I asked my mom, and her response was not at all, just what I expected her to say. She explained that my Nanny (Grandmom), her mother, had been in foster care with her siblings when she was a child. My Nanny's experience was not good, and my mother wanted to change that for other children in foster care. My parents had raised all four of us and many of our cousins along the way, so I figured their experience was enough for the task. I will not pretend that I was all in on the idea at first; it was difficult enough to share my parents with my siblings, let alone other children. This was far more important than I was.

They accepted their first child and it seemed like children just keep rolling in. Before you knew it, they had fostered about 100 children. Each child became part of our extended family. I know you should not have favorites but as human beings, you do not always have control over your emotions. Nickema, Jaquan, and Richard, will always hold a special place in my heart.

I began to do respite care for my parents and sister who had become a foster parent after doing respite care for our parents and eventually I became a foster parent myself. I did both Treatment Foster Care and Caminos Foster Care. The Caminos Program is different because the children placed in your care are from different countries. Often the children do not speak English and have no family members in the United States. They are struggling with both language and culture, not to mention the trauma related to their journey to the United States and time spent in holding centers. Keep in mind these are children. However, fostering for these children means that foster parents must familiarize themselves with the child's culture. This will help to bridge the gap between the two cultures as well as help the child to retain his/her culture. It means ensuring a connection with their families, which often includes younger siblings. These children must endure Immigration Courts and the uncertainty of their future. Children often riddled with anxiety and insomnia. As with all children, they need trust and a feeling of belonging. What you get in return is immeasurable.

Being a foster parent is challenging work and some days you want to give up. However, if you muster through and fight as if they are yours, you will succeed, and they will know that there is someone in this world willing to fight for them.

Karmentrina Schevelle Kearse, Daughter of the Author

Aaron and Sandra Stockton